God Calls You Worthy

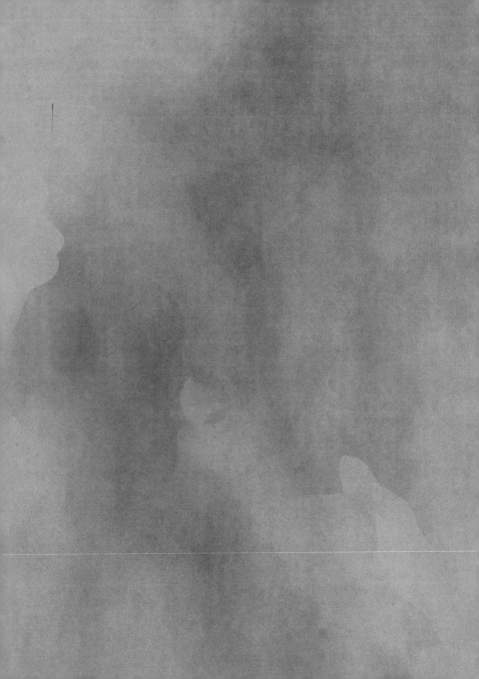

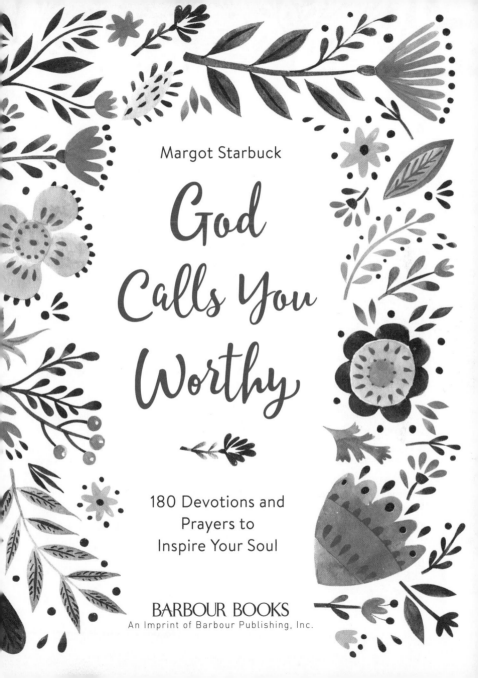

Margot Starbuck

God Calls You Worthy

180 Devotions and
Prayers to
Inspire Your Soul

BARBOUR BOOKS
An Imprint of Barbour Publishing, Inc.

ISBN 978-1-64352-474-0

Published by Barbour Books, an imprint of Barbour Publishing, Inc., 1810 Barbour Drive, Uhrichsville, Ohio 44683, www.barbourbooks.com

Our mission is to inspire the world with the life-changing message of the Bible.

ecpa Member of the Evangelical Christian Publishers Association

Printed in China.

"Because I am God, your personal God,
The Holy of Israel, your Savior.
I paid a huge price for you: all of Egypt,
with rich Cush and Seba thrown in!
That's how much you mean to me!
That's how much I love you!
I'd sell off the whole world to get you back,
trade the creation just for you."
Isaiah 43:3–4 MSG

Many of us wonder, in our deep places, whether we are worthy of love, both human and divine. And the enemy capitalizes on our wondering by hissing naughty words in our ears. "You're not *really* worth knowing. You're not *really* worth loving."

But throughout scripture we hear another voice that shouts, "I paid a huge price for you. . . ! *That's* how much you mean to Me! *That's* how much I love you!" And as we discover the inherent value that God has assigned to each of us, we also discover that it has nothing to do with what we're bringing to the table—our faithfulness, our goodness, our works—and everything to do with a good Creator and what Christ has done for us. God is the One who has made us inherently worthy of love.

God Calls You Worthy has been written to remind you daily that you are entirely and irrevocably worthy of love. The 180 scriptures, devotions, and brief prayers can nourish you as you purpose to live in the truth of who God says you are.

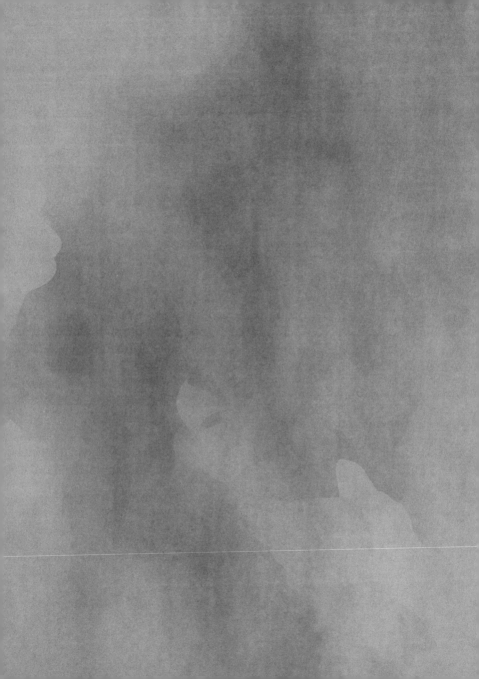

Named by God

As he says in Hosea: "I will call them 'my people' who are not my people; and I will call her 'my loved one' who is not my loved one," and, "In the very place where it was said to them, 'You are not my people,' there they will be called 'children of the living God.' "

ROMANS 9:25–26

Did you know that God addresses you as *who you really are*? The meaning of the names of two of Hosea's children were "not loved" and "not my people." But God changed their names to "my loved one" and "children of the living God." Isn't that beautiful? If we've faced hurt, or abuse, or neglect in the past, we may be carrying a name in our hearts that lies about who we really are. In our deep places, some of us have carried the name "rejected" or "abandoned," "forgotten" or "unloved." But God's Spirit gently whispers to the ears of our hearts what is most true about who we are. When we listen to God's voice, we hear the names: *accepted, pursued, cherished, beloved.* Offer God the particularities of your story, and listen for the true word God speaks about who you are.

Lord, I want to hear Your voice that speaks only truth. Uproot the names that lie about my worth, and replace them with the true names You have for me. Speak, Lord, for Your servant is listening. Amen.

Created Very Good

Let them praise the name of the Lord, for at his command they were created, and he established them for ever and ever—he issued a decree that will never pass away.
Psalm 148:5–6

If you went to a painting class, the teacher might have you re-create a painting by Van Gogh of sunflowers in a vase. You may or may not create a convincing imitation. Maybe a counterfeiter of classic paintings was working beside you and actually crafted a piece that was indistinguishable from Van Gogh's original. No matter how close the copy comes to the original, though, it will never be as valuable as the one created through the hands, mind, and heart of Vincent van Gogh. The same is true of you. No matter how you believe you came into the world, you were crafted by the Master Creator. You were lovingly sculpted as a one-of-a-kind original that no one can ever copy. You are of inestimable worth because you bear the thumbprint of your Maker, reflecting the very image of God. As a result, you are worthy beyond measure.

God, help the truth of who You are and who I am to penetrate my heart. I believe that You are my Maker and that I reflect Your goodness and Your glory. Today I live in the truth that I am incomparably worthy because of You. Amen.

You Are Loved as Jesus Was Loved

"As the Father has loved me, so have I loved you. Now remain in my love. If you keep my commands, you will remain in my love, just as I have kept my Father's commands and remain in his love. I have told you this so that my joy may be in you and that your joy may be complete. My command is this: Love each other as I have loved you."

JOHN 15:9–12

It's no secret that there are all different kinds of love in the world. Women love their friends. Children love their favorite toys. Mothers love their infants. And some of us really *really* love chocolate. Even in scripture, the original languages use different words for "love." One is a kind of brotherly or sisterly love. One is a passionate, romantic love. And another is a selfless true love for another. Before He leaves them, Jesus assures His followers that they are loved. But He's very clear that it's not at all in an "I love ice cream" or "I love my bro" kind of way. No, Jesus promises that the way He loves us is *exactly* the way His Father loved Him. Amazing, right?

Jesus, I believe that Your words are true. Thank You that Your love for me is perfect. Today, help me perceive and receive the great love You have for me. Amen.

God Hears Your Voice

The Lord is far from the wicked, but he hears the prayer of the righteous. Light in a messenger's eyes brings joy to the heart, and good news gives health to the bones. Whoever heeds life-giving correction will be at home among the wise.

Proverbs 15:29–31

Have you ever felt utterly alone? Maybe it was in the wake of a scary medical diagnosis. Or after you were hurt or abused by someone you trusted. Perhaps you felt abandoned when your marriage ended. Or you may have felt alone when you lost a parent or other loved one to death. When we face these kinds of crises and traumas, the enemy capitalizes on our experience by hissing to our hearts that we are alone. The one who lies can even convince us that we are not seen. Not heard. Not loved. But the voice that lies does not have the final word in our lives. Scripture promises that God hears the prayers of the righteous. God sees your tears. God hears your voice. The One who loves you is attentive to every word you pray silently and aloud. Today, know and believe that *you are heard* by God.

God, today I am choosing to trust the promise I read in Your Word. And because I am confident that You hear my voice, I will speak to You throughout the day. God, thank You for listening to my prayers. Amen.

You Are among a Chosen People

But you are a chosen people, a royal priesthood, a holy nation, God's special possession, that you may declare the praises of him who called you out of darkness into his wonderful light.
1 Peter 2:9

Remember when you were in high school? If you attended a public or private high school, you probably remember that there were kids who were a part of the "in" group and those who were on the "outs." And if you were homeschooled, you've certainly caught on to the way schools work from every movie featuring teenagers ever! Beyond social cliques, there were tryouts for the basketball team, for cheerleading, for the gymnastics squad, or for show choir. In so many kinds of situations, you were either "chosen" or you were "unchosen." A letter Peter wrote to early believers identifies them as a people who were chosen as God's special possession. And because you are Jesus' own, you're included as well. Yes, it's a blessing to you to be in God's family. But Peter's clear that as someone who's chosen, you're called to invite others into God's wonderful light. Today, live as one who is God's own, and welcome others into the family.

God, because of Jesus Christ, I am included as one of Your chosen people. And I do not take that blessing for granted. Fill me with Your light today so that I might share it with others. Amen.

The Lord Has Received Me

Though my father and mother forsake me, the Lord will receive me. Teach me your way, Lord; lead me in a straight path because of my oppressors.
Psalm 27:10–11

If you're like most people, your experience of family is imperfect. (Okay, if you're like *all* people!) Maybe your conception was unexpected. Perhaps you were relinquished for adoption at birth. Maybe you lived in a home with violence. Or maybe you had parents who did the best they could to meet your needs, but they still failed to love you as you needed to be loved. Because there is only One capable of loving us with a perfect love, many of us have arrived in adulthood with bumps and scrapes and scars from the first few decades of our lives. The psalmist identifies that reality by praying, "Though my father and mother forsake me, the Lord will receive me." As we consider some of the hurts we endured in our families, God invites us to turn our faces toward the One who cannot fail. As we offer ourselves to God, we discover that we are received completely by the Father who loves us.

Father, Your Word assures me that I am worth loving. I thank You that You love me with a perfect love that does not fail. Today, I choose to trust in Your love. Amen.

God Loved You First

This is love: not that we loved God, but that he loved us and sent his Son as an atoning sacrifice for our sins. Dear friends, since God so loved us, we also ought to love one another. No one has ever seen God; but if we love one another, God lives in us and his love is made complete in us.

1 John 4:10–12

What is the story you tell of becoming a member of God's family? Maybe you were born into a Christian family, baptized as an infant, and raised in the faith. Perhaps you came to know God's big love for you as a teenager and accepted Jesus as your Savior. Or maybe you only recognized your need for God's love and forgiveness when your life crumbled and you realized you couldn't do it on your own anymore. Whenever we come to know God, it can be tempting to believe that we somehow discovered God and chose to love Him. While that may be true, it's even more true that before we were conceived, and before we prayed a prayer for salvation, or before we stood at the front of church to declare our faith, *God loved us first.*

God, I confess that I'm tempted to believe that my faith depends on my love for You. And I thank You for Your Word that assures me that You loved me first, and You continue to love me. Amen.

God Never Leaves You

"The Lord himself goes before you and will be with you; he will never leave you nor forsake you. Do not be afraid; do not be discouraged."
Deuteronomy 31:8

Have you heard the story about footprints in the sand? A person reviews the journey of the life they've lived and is a bit miffed by what's revealed. Although God was often accompanying the person through the joyful parts of the journey—revealed by two sets of footprints on the beach—during the most difficult seasons, there was only one set of footprints. Feel familiar? Have you ever felt abandoned by God? Raising a fist to God during those hard seasons, we can be tempted to rail, "Hey, God, what gives?! Why have You left me now?!" And like the beach walker, God reminds us that those are the seasons when God was carrying us! In the most difficult parts of our journeys, we can feel forsaken by God. As hard as we look and listen for God's presence, it can be difficult to discern where God is in our lives. But God's Word promises us that God never leaves us or forsakes us. *Particularly* in our hardest days.

God, no matter what I face, I will not fear. I am not discouraged because I am confident that You are with me. Lord, remind me throughout this day of Your steadfast, faithful presence with me. Amen.

You Are My Beloved

When all the people were being baptized, Jesus was baptized too. And as he was praying, heaven was opened and the Holy Spirit descended on him in bodily form like a dove. And a voice came from heaven: "You are my Son, whom I love; with you I am well pleased."

Luke 3:21–22

A lot of us are tempted to earn affirmation in ways that never quite truly satisfy. We may join every club and committee in our churches and communities and still never feel like we belong. Or maybe we've sought love in relationships that weren't God's best for us. Or perhaps we tried to prove our worth through our work or achievements but still never felt like we could do enough to be worthy. At Jesus' baptism, the voice of His Father affirmed His belonging, His belovedness, and His worth by saying, "You are my Son, whom I love; with you I am well pleased." While God was specifically identifying Jesus as the One who would redeem the world, God is kind and faithful to remind each one of us that we are God's daughters and that we are beloved and that God is pleased with us.

Father, I confess that I'm tempted to try to earn Your love. But just as You offered it freely to Jesus, You offer it freely to me. Today, let me receive Your unfailing love. Amen.

God Comforts Me as a Beloved Child

For this is what the Lord says: "I will extend peace to her like a river, and the wealth of nations like a flooding stream; you will nurse and be carried on her arm and dandled on her knees. As a mother comforts her child, so will I comfort you; and you will be comforted over Jerusalem."

Isaiah 66:12–13

Have you ever watched a mother comfort a young child who's hurt or afraid? If her infant is hungry or distressed, she may offer her breast for nursing. If a boy or girl has fallen, a mother might scoop her child into her arms, cradling the child in love. If a child is scared, she might place the child on her knee, look into her eyes, and reassure her that she is safe. When God's people were distressed, the prophet Isaiah assured them that God was the kind of mother to nurse and hold and comfort. If you've experienced this kind of tender care from a mother or grandmother or other caregiver, you may still be able to feel that comfort in your body. And if your caregivers weren't resourced to offer you what you needed, you might close your eyes and see God as your perfect comforter.

God, it can feel like a stretch to know You as a comforting mother, but I believe that Your Word is true. Comfort my heart with Your love. Amen.

You Are Worthy of Care

"And why do you worry about clothes? See how the flowers of the field grow. They do not labor or spin. Yet I tell you that not even Solomon in all his splendor was dressed like one of these. If that is how God clothes the grass of the field, which is here today and tomorrow is thrown into the fire, will he not much more clothe you—you of little faith?"

MATTHEW 6:28–30

When we listen in on what Jesus taught His first followers, it's obvious that Jesus understood the human heart. He knew what kinds of concerns occupy our minds. If we're underresourced, we worry about affording the clothes that we need. If we're well resourced, we worry about finding the clothes that we want. But when Jesus speaks to us, He wants us to understand the Father's heart toward us. He wants us to know that God, who clothes the fields in a beautiful array of flowers, knows what we need. God cares what we need. God provides what we need. Jesus wants His followers to know for certain that His Father is our good provider.

God, I confess that I have wasted energy worrying about what I want and need. But today I lift my eyes toward You because I believe Jesus' assurance that I am Yours and that I am worthy of Your care. Amen.

God Has Given Me Purpose

The word of the Lord came to me, saying, "Before I formed you in the womb I knew you, before you were born I set you apart; I appointed you as a prophet to the nations." "Alas, Sovereign Lord," I said, "I do not know how to speak; I am too young." But the Lord said to me, "Do not say, 'I am too young.' You must go to everyone I send you to and say whatever I command you."

Jeremiah 1:4–7

You are discovering that you are worthy of God's attention. God's care. God's love. And you're also discovering that God has created you for a purpose. God has given you gifts, passions, talents, and abilities to be used to build the kingdom on earth as it is in heaven. Just as God formed Jeremiah in the womb of his mother, the Lord also knit you together in the secret place. And God chose you to serve Him. Even when you've glimpsed what it is God has called you to do, you may still be tempted to balk. But you are worthy and you are equipped not because of your own merit but because of God's. You need not be afraid because God is your helper!

God, I believe that You have made me and equipped me for a particular purpose. As You continue to show me what that purpose is, embolden me today to do what You've made me to do. Amen.

Feed Me Today, Lord

"For the bread of God is the bread that comes down from heaven and gives life to the world." "Sir," they said, "always give us this bread." Then Jesus declared, "I am the bread of life. Whoever comes to me will never go hungry, and whoever believes in me will never be thirsty."

JOHN 6:33–35

Although bread's gotten a bit of a bad rap in recent culinary history, where so many of us have been taught to despise carbs, in the ancient world, bread was a symbol of life. Carbs aside, bread represents the daily provision we need to survive and to thrive. And Jesus revealed to His hungry followers that He was the bread that comes down from heaven to give life to the world. That announcement was a lot for them to wrap their minds around, and it can be for us today as well. So Jesus makes it plain to them and to us: "*Whoever comes to me will never go hungry, and whoever believes in me will never be thirsty.*" So, what is the deep need of your heart today? Do you need to be fed physically? Emotionally? Spiritually? As you tip your eyes and ears toward Jesus, He promises to meet the deep needs of your heart.

Jesus, You know exactly what it is that I need today. And I trust that You are a good provider. Show me how to receive what You provide. Amen.

I Seek Your Wisdom

Prudence is a fountain of life to the prudent, but folly brings punishment to fools. The hearts of the wise make their mouths prudent, and their lips promote instruction. Gracious words are a honeycomb, sweet to the soul and healing to the bones.

PROVERBS 16:22–24

As you think about the people God has put in your life, which one do you believe possesses *wisdom*? Hold that person now in your heart and mind. Although I don't know who that person is, I feel confident venturing a guess that she or he is someone whose *words* give life. I'd guess that this is a person who shares wise, life-giving words with others who are a blessing, and I'd venture a guess that this person knows when to remain silent, rejecting opportunities to criticize, gossip, or condemn. Beloved, God has created you and equipped you to use your words for good. Today, you can choose prudence, choose wisdom, choose life by allowing God's Spirit to guide the words you speak—words that are "sweet to the soul and healing to the bones."

Lord, I confess that I can be careless with my words. So, today I commit myself to be Your faithful servant. Fill my heart, my mind, and my mouth with words that give life to others, so that You might be glorified. Amen.

Offer Mercy as One Who's Received Mercy

"Blessed are the merciful, for they will be shown mercy. Blessed are the pure in heart, for they will see God. Blessed are the peacemakers, for they will be called children of God. Blessed are those who are persecuted because of righteousness, for theirs is the kingdom of heaven."

MATTHEW 5:7–10

A friend has known the Lord for years, but she still struggles to believe she is worthy of mercy and forgiveness. If you know someone like this, you may also know the personal suffering that comes from being afflicted in this way. But in the end, she might actually be right! We have been shown mercy not because we are worthy but because God is merciful. We've received God's great love for us, which was demonstrated through Jesus. And as people who have received great mercy, we are called to extend mercy to others. One of the ways to live into what God has done for us is to extend God's grace to others. Is there someone you don't feel like forgiving? As you extend mercy and grace to that one, you might even experience God's grace in a new way as you share it with others.

Father, today I choose to receive Your great love and mercy for me. As I do, help me to offer that good gift to others. Make me a vessel of Your care for others. Amen.

Love Is as Strong as Death

Place me like a seal over your heart, like a seal on your arm; for love is as strong as death, its jealousy unyielding as the grave. It burns like blazing fire, like a mighty flame.

Song of Songs 8:6

Every one of us is born with a natural fear of death. For some of us, that's expressed by wisely avoiding dangerous situations. Others may struggle emotionally when it's time to visit a loved one in a hospital or at a nursing care facility. And others may have a conscious fear of death that plagues their minds. The enemy of our souls wants to convince us that death will win. But in Jesus, God has turned death on its head. In Jesus' resurrection, not only was His story rewritten, but ours was as well. We have seen with our eyes that God's love conquers the power of death. We have the assurance that just as the grave was not the end for Jesus, it is not the end for us. We also know that, moment by moment, God's love frees us from death's grip. Today, God's love wins.

Lord, I feel the pull of death's power in my life. But I also trust the promise of Your Word that love is as strong as death. Through the power of Your Holy Spirit, free me today from death's grip. Amen.

You Are Inestimably Worthy

He said to them, "If any of you has a sheep and it falls into a pit on the Sabbath, will you not take hold of it and lift it out? How much more valuable is a person than a sheep! Therefore it is lawful to do good on the Sabbath."
MATTHEW 12:11–12

God's law prohibited Jews from doing work on the Sabbath. When Jesus healed people on the Sabbath—a form of work—the religious leaders gave Him a lot of flak for it. But in this instance and in so many others, Jesus demonstrated that the law of love is God's highest authority. Jesus knew that if one of these religious leaders had a sheep that fell into a ditch on the Sabbath, the value of that property would compel them to do the work of dragging it out of that ditch—and no one would have faulted them for it. And Jesus wanted His hearers to know that a beloved individual created by God ought to be healed on the Sabbath because she or he has *inestimable* worth. Beloved, that's you! You are altogether worthy in God's sight. When you live into that reality, you agree with what God has declared is most true about who you are.

God, I believe that I am precious and worthy of Your care.
In Your eyes, I am more valuable than I can even imagine.
Today, help me to live as Your beloved daughter. Amen.

God Is with You Today

David also said to Solomon his son, "Be strong and courageous, and do the work. Do not be afraid or discouraged, for the Lord God, my God, is with you. He will not fail you or forsake you until all the work for the service of the temple of the Lord is finished."

1 Chronicles 28:20

Have you ever had a clear sense of what God has created you to do? Maybe you know that the Lord has called you to create—with paint, with clay, with sounds, with words. Or maybe you have a strong sense of calling to a particular group of people: children, soldiers, immigrants, athletes, or people with disabilities. Or perhaps your calling in this season is to care for the needs of a particular family member. Solomon had a very clear directive from God to build the temple, and his father, David, encouraged him to keep trusting God as he did that work. Today, David's confident faith can speak into your particular calling as well: "Do not be afraid or discouraged, for the Lord God, my God, is with you." Sister, you were made for a purpose, and today God will strengthen you to fulfill that purpose.

Lord, I put my trust in You. As I consider the work for which You have made me and to which You have called me, I seek Your help today. Give me wisdom and strength to accomplish Your will. Amen.

Having Faith to Ask

Throwing his cloak aside, he jumped to his feet and came to Jesus. "What do you want me to do for you?" Jesus asked him. The blind man said, "Rabbi, I want to see." "Go," said Jesus, "your faith has healed you." Immediately he received his sight and followed Jesus along the road.

Mark 10:50–52

When an infant cries, her parent learns to discern whether she is hungry, wet, or tired. Recognizing the child's need, the parent gladly meets the need. As that child grows a bit older and learns to speak, the parent teaches the child to *say* what it is that she wants or needs. Their relationship is strengthened as the child asks and the parent meets the need. When Jesus encountered the man who was blind, He *knew* what the man needed. But He invited the man into relationship with Him by asking, "What do you want me to do for you?" By asking for what he needed and wanted, the man who was blind expressed his faith that Jesus, the Rabbi, had the power to heal him. Today what is it that you want and need from Jesus? As you name it and boldly ask Jesus to meet your need, your relationship with Him is strengthened.

Jesus, I confess that I am often afraid to ask You for what I most want and need. Forgive me. Today, I will ask You with boldness, confident that You are the giver of all good gifts. Amen.

You Are Altogether Worthy

So God created mankind in his own image, in the image of God he created them; male and female he created them.
Genesis 1:27

In the ancient world, a king was believed to bear, or reflect, the image of the deity on whose behalf he reigned. For instance, King David would have been thought to reflect the image of the God of Israel. So, when God's Word says that each individual in the human race reflects the image of God, that's a pretty big deal! Of course, it includes *you*. Across the centuries, since Genesis was written, theologians have had different opinions about what it means to reflect the image of God. Some believe God's image is reflected in our human capacity to reason. Others have believed it is our ability to be creative and to create. And others think that we reflect God's image by our capacity for relationship. There are several ways that you and I reflect, for the world, who God is. One thing is certain: because you bear the holy imprint of God's image, you are altogether undeniably worthy.

God, the voices around me tell me that I am not enough: not pretty enough, not fit enough, not smart enough, not accomplished enough. But Your Word says that I am altogether worthy because I bear Your image. Today, I accept the truth of my worth in You. Amen.

You Are Entirely New

So from now on we regard no one from a worldly point of view. Though we once regarded Christ in this way, we do so no longer. Therefore, if anyone is in Christ, the new creation has come: The old has gone, the new is here!
2 Corinthians 5:16–17

When Paul wrote to believers in the early church, he wanted them to understand their unique identity as followers of Jesus. He reminded them that anyone who is in Christ is a *new creation*. Paul knew that they, and we, would need to be reminded of who we really are: children who are redeemed by God and worthy of God's love. But daily the enemy whispers in our ear, "You haven't *really* changed. You haven't *really* been redeemed by God. You're not *really* worthy of God's grace and love." But when we stand on God's Word, we answer the enemy's wily lies with what is most true: "I am a new creation, and I am worthy of God's love."

Father, I have heard the voice of the enemy hissing that I am still the old creation I once was: guilty, ashamed, unworthy, unloved. But today, through the power of Your Word, I claim what is most true about who I am because of who You are. I am a new creation in Christ. Amen.

God Gives You Courage

And pray in the Spirit on all occasions with all kinds of prayers and requests. With this in mind, be alert and always keep on praying for all the Lord's people. Pray also for me, that whenever I speak, words may be given me so that I will fearlessly make known the mystery of the gospel.

EPHESIANS 6:18–19

You matter to God. Not only do you matter to God, but God has given you a kingdom assignment that only you can do. Paul understood that his particular assignment was to proclaim the good news of the Gospel with the words God had given him. God has also given you gifts to be used in the building of His kingdom. Maybe you have a heart for elderly folks in your community. Or adolescents. Or perhaps God's called you to be a friend to those with intellectual disabilities. Whatever it is that God has called you to do, God will equip you to do it! When you pray, God gives you all you need to work fearlessly to establish His kingdom on earth as it is in heaven.

God, I confess that I can be slow to use the gifts that You have given me. I feel like I don't have what it takes to serve You faithfully. Give me courage to be the woman You created me to be and to use my gifts to love and serve others in Your name. Amen.

Praise God with All You Are

Shout for joy to the LORD, all the earth, burst into jubilant song with music; make music to the LORD with the harp, with the harp and the sound of singing, with trumpets and the blast of the ram's horn—shout for joy before the LORD, the King.

PSALM 98:4–6

Have you ever worshipped God halfheartedly? Your mind is distracted. Your voice is weak. Your spirit is tired. It can be tempting for those of us who worship God regularly to fall into a rut with our worship, going through rote motions without giving God our best. But the psalmist's wholehearted worship reminds us that God is worthy of all we have to give. This week, how can you adjust your worship to celebrate God with all you are? Maybe you'll clap your hands or lift your arms to the Lord as you worship. Or maybe you'll pick up an instrument at home—an old guitar, keyboard, or maraca—to worship God with joy and gladness. Or maybe you'll even turn on your favorite music and dance before God! This week, worship the Lord with all that you are.

Lord, You are King of heaven and earth! I offer You my mind and my voice and my body as I worship You. May my worship be pleasing in Your sight. Amen.

Experience God's Unfathomable Peace

Rejoice in the Lord always. I will say it again: Rejoice! Let your gentleness be evident to all. The Lord is near. Do not be anxious about anything, but in every situation, by prayer and petition, with thanksgiving, present your requests to God. And the peace of God, which transcends all understanding, will guard your hearts and your minds in Christ Jesus.

PHILIPPIANS 4:4–7

Daily we can be tempted to let anxiety and worry creep into our hearts and minds. When we wake up, an ache or pain triggers worries about our health. Within a few hours, we're feeling anxious about financial obligations. Through the day, we obsess about the plight of a loved one. And by evening, we're consumed with worry about either our singleness or our married-ness! But God's Word promises each of us a peace that is larger than our circumstances. When we pray, thanking God for what we have and asking God for what we need, we have the privilege of releasing every one of our cares to God. Beloved, know that God cares for you. The Lord is near to you this day, and He can be trusted with all the cares you hold in your heart.

God, my heart is heavy with worries I have for myself, my family, and others. Some are small and some are bigger than I am! Lord, I release these concerns to You and open myself to receive the peace You promise. Amen.

Saved by Grace

It is by grace you have been saved, through faith—
and this is not from yourselves, it is the gift of God—
not by works, so that no one can boast.
EPHESIANS 2:8–9

Even though we know that Jesus saved us because He loves us, it can be really tempting to think that our faith depends on our good works. We slip into that trap when we believe that God is pleased with us because we spent hours in prayer, served at church, or shared the Gospel with a stranger. While those actions no doubt delight God's heart, our salvation doesn't depend on them. And here comes the really fantastic news: that assurance also means that when we fail, when we sin against God in small ways and big ones, we're *still* saved by God's grace. Isn't that great news? Regardless of your performance, God has you.

God, thank You for the assurance that I am held in Your loving grace even when I fail. I am grateful that my salvation depends on You and not on me! Father, I am humbled by Your grace. Amen.

The One Who Has Made God Known

Out of his fullness we have all received grace in place of grace already given. For the law was given through Moses; grace and truth came through Jesus Christ. No one has ever seen God, but the one and only Son, who is himself God and is in closest relationship with the Father, has made him known.

John 1:16–18

Around the globe and across different cultures, there are countless opinions about who God is. Various writings and prophets have claimed to hold the truth about the identity and character of God. But the Bible and the Gospels in particular make a pretty audacious claim about God's identity. John says that there is one person who's made God known, and this is "the one and only Son." What John is saying is that we discover who God is when we know who Jesus is. When we see Jesus pursuing a disreputable and unscrupulous tax collector, we know what God is like. When we hear Jesus weeping with Martha at the death of her brother, we know what God is like. When we taste the bread Jesus feeds to five thousand, we know what God is like. And today, Jesus is still making the Father known!

God, I believe the testimony of John and others that assures me Jesus has made You known. Open the eyes and ears of my heart today so I can see Your face and hear Your voice. Amen.

Faithful to Generations—and Me

Lord, you have been our dwelling place throughout all generations. Before the mountains were born or you brought forth the whole world, from everlasting to everlasting you are God.

Psalm 90:1–2

When we form friendships, we learn whether we can trust someone by the way we see them behave. If a friend fails to show up for us, shares our secrets, or harms us, we discover that she's not trustworthy. But if a friend listens well, keeps our confidence, and loves us consistently, we learn that we can trust her. And we know that we can trust God because the Bible gives us a written record of how God has related to His people throughout the generations. When God's people suffered in Egypt, God rescued them. When they hungered in the desert, He fed them. When they wandered, He led them. And in Jesus we see in the flesh the One who redeems and feeds and leads. The God who has loved His children with a steadfast, faithful love throughout the centuries is the same One who's available to shelter you today. The God of Abraham, Isaac, Jesus, and Paul can be trusted!

God, I see the ways You have faithfully cared for Your people throughout the generations. You are reliable. You are steadfast. You are gracious. Lord, I trust You with my life today. Amen.

Keep Yourself in God's Love

But you, dear friends, by building yourselves up in your most holy faith and praying in the Holy Spirit, keep yourselves in God's love as you wait for the mercy of our Lord Jesus Christ to bring you to eternal life.

Jude 20–21

Have you ever shown up to church on Sunday and realized that your entire week zipped by without you ever once pausing to notice God's face or listen for God's voice? (Don't worry, you're not alone!) The demands of the world—our jobs, families, friends, homes, and responsibilities—all vie for our time and attention. But God has something much better for us. Toward the end of the New Testament, a little letter from a servant named Jude exhorts believers to "keep yourselves in God's love." Isn't that a beautiful image? When you snuggle up in bed tonight, you might imagine God's love wrapping and enfolding you like your sheet or cozy blanket. Daily we can choose to remain in God's love. Maybe upon waking in the morning or hitting the pillow at night, we breathe a prayer: "I am held in God's love."

Lord, I confess that too often I attempt to live independently of Your love, Your grace, Your care. Forgive me. This week I choose to keep myself in Your love as I wait for Jesus. Remind me daily that I am held by Your love. Amen.

You Saw My Affliction

I will be glad and rejoice in your love, for you saw my affliction and knew the anguish of my soul. You have not given me into the hands of the enemy but have set my feet in a spacious place.
Psalm 31:7–8

When our souls are troubled, we can often feel very lonely. Suffering a failure at work, we feel ashamed. Weathering a romantic disappointment, we feel isolated. Enduring the consequences of a sinful choice we've made, we feel guilty. Throbbing from hurts of the past, we feel deep sadness. And sometimes we can even feel lonely and isolated when we're surrounded by people who love us. And in these painful moments and seasons, the enemy of our soul lies: "You are not seen. You are not heard. You are not loved." But when the psalmist was afflicted, the writer recognized God's steadfast, faithful presence. In the midst of darkness, truth announced, "I see your affliction. I know the anguish of your soul." In our anguish, we are never alone.

God, my circumstances and my emotions make me feel alone. And the deceiver insists that I am unseen and unheard. But I put my faith in Your Word that promises You will never leave me or forsake me. Today I am seen. Today I am heard. Today I am known and loved by You. Thank You for that assurance. Amen.

You Are Worth Pursuing

"Then he calls his friends and neighbors together and says, 'Rejoice with me; I have found my lost sheep.' I tell you that in the same way there will be more rejoicing in heaven over one sinner who repents than over ninety-nine righteous persons who do not need to repent."

Luke 15:6–7

In some of the very best rom coms, it can begin to look as though the girl is not going to win the heart of her man. But if the movie is worth its salt, before those final credits roll, his eyes will be opened—he'll see how worthy she is, and he'll work to earn her love. The plot appeals because the deep longing of every heart is to be seen, known, pursued, and loved. This is exactly the kind of love Jesus describes His Father having for us. The lover of our souls drops everything to pursue us, rejoicing when we're finally found. Spend some time with this story, and let the reality of God's extravagant love for you soak into your deep places. You are the prize, and your redemption causes God's heart to rejoice.

Lord, all around me are voices whispering that I'm not really worth pursuing or loving. And some of my experience also resonates with that lie! But I believe Jesus' assurance that You are the One who pursues me because I am beloved and precious to You. Thank You for Your love. Amen.

God Redeems

"Then you, my people, will know that I am the LORD, when I open your graves and bring you up from them. I will put my Spirit in you and you will live, and I will settle you in your own land. Then you will know that I the LORD have spoken, and I have done it, declares the LORD."

EZEKIEL 37:13–14

In the book of Ezekiel, the prophet and God take a pretty unusual field trip together. The Lord led Ezekiel into a valley filled with dry bones as far as the eye could see. He was encircled by death. And God asked Ezekiel, "Can these bones live?" (Ezekiel 37:3). How would you have answered? It's entirely apparent to the naked eye that death has defeated whatever once lived. But Ezekiel spit out the most diplomatic reply, "Sovereign LORD, you alone know." (Nice one, E.) What Ezekiel would learn, and what we've learned from the resurrection of Jesus, is that God is in the business of bringing life out of death. In the most unlikely circumstances, God defeats the power of death and brings forth something new. Where is the death in your life that God wants to redeem?

God, give me Your vision today. Because of Jesus, I know that You can bring what is dead to life. Lord, I offer You the parts of my life where there is death. Defeat. Decay. I release them into Your care because I trust that You are a faithful Redeemer. Amen.

You Are Worth Protecting

"My prayer is not that you take them out of the world but that you protect them from the evil one. They are not of the world, even as I am not of it. Sanctify them by the truth; your word is truth. As you sent me into the world, I have sent them into the world. For them I sanctify myself, that they too may be truly sanctified."

John 17:15–19

Chances are high, 100 percent in fact, that you grew up in an imperfect family. No matter how much your parents or caregivers loved you, they were—by nature—imperfect people. Because a father is imperfect, he may have hurt you by his absence or by his presence. Because a mother is imperfect, she may have inadvertently or purposefully harmed you. Because every caregiver is *human*, they weren't always able and equipped to give you what you most needed. But Jesus' prayer to the Father for you is "Protect them." Nearing the end of His life, He begs God, "Protect them from the evil one." Beloved, believe that you are *worth* protecting. Even when those around you were not able to do it well, you are inherently worthy of being protected.

God, You know the hurts of my heart. You are aware of the moments when I was not protected from the schemes of the enemy. Today, believing I am worthy, I seek Your healing and rest in Your care. Amen.

The Lord Hears You

How long will you people turn my glory into shame? How long will you love delusions and seek false gods? Know that the LORD *has set apart his faithful servant for himself; the* LORD *hears when I call to him.*

PSALM 4:2–3

Daily we're surrounded by messages convincing us that we will find happiness in things that can't really satisfy our souls. We're willing to believe that if we had a spouse, a better spouse, a better job, a better house, a better *second* house, *then* we could finally be satisfied. If we had her body or his money or their kids, then we'd be happy. And when we see the smiling selfies on social media, it's easy to believe! But the psalmist reminds us that we are tempted to pursue false gods. We seek that which, ultimately, cannot satisfy. But we're assured that the faithful servant, who's not chasing after delusions, is set apart for God. And when we call, God *hears* us. Taking our eyes off the world's false promises and lifting our eyes and voices to God, we find what we most need.

Lord, I confess that I am tempted to seek happiness in all kinds of ways. You know the particular temptations of my heart. Forgive me. Today I set my eyes on You, and I listen for Your voice. Amen.

This Is Your Mission

"A new command I give you: Love one another. As I have loved you, so you must love one another. By this everyone will know that you are my disciples, if you love one another."
JOHN 13:34–35

After Jesus had walked with His disciples for three years, He prepared Himself *and them* for what was to come. Although *they* didn't understand His impending absence, He knew that He had only a little time left with them. Like the parent dropping off a child at college or the kind grandfather dispensing wisdom at his grandchild's wedding, He wanted to make sure that they knew *how to live*. They'd heard His teachings, they'd watched how He lived, and He wanted to equip them to live well in His absence. He wanted them to understand the most important thing about being His followers. He boiled it down to three words: "Love one another." In essence, He was saying, "You've watched Me do it, you've experienced My love for you, so that's how I want you to love each other." Jesus boiled down His teachings for His earliest disciples and for us, and today the world recognizes Him in the way we love one another.

Father, teach me to love like Jesus loved. As I study Your Word and seek His face, infuse me with Your Spirit so that I might love others the way Jesus has loved me. Amen.

Made for a Purpose

The word of the Lord came to me, saying, "Before I formed you in the womb I knew you, before you were born I set you apart; I appointed you as a prophet to the nations."
Jeremiah 1:4–5

Have you ever experienced that wonderful feeling of knowing that you were doing the thing for which you were made? Being the person you were created to be? Perhaps you felt it when you were serving someone else close to home or farther away. Or maybe you knew you were being who God made you to be when you were knitting a baby blanket, composing a song, or creating a painting. Or you might have felt that holy sense of purpose when you were sharing one of your passions with others. Just as God had a special purpose for Jeremiah before he was even formed in his mother's womb, God has a purpose for you. And what's critical to remember is that your purpose is *unique*! Too often we can get stuck wishing that we had another woman's gifts, talents, or calling. But because God created you to be entirely unique, your special purpose will be as well. When you pray, notice the particular gifts and passions with which God has entrusted *you*.

Lord, I believe that You have created me with a special purpose. Continue to show me how I can faithfully use what You have given me so that Your kingdom might be built on earth as it is in heaven. Amen.

In Life and Death, We Belong to God

For none of us lives for ourselves alone, and none of us dies for ourselves alone. If we live, we live for the Lord; and if we die, we die for the Lord. So, whether we live or die, we belong to the Lord.

ROMANS 14:7–8

The fear of death drives us in ways we may not even realize. We color our faces and our hair to present the illusion that we are not aging. We pay thousands of dollars to doctors and surgeons who sculpt us to appear as though we're not nearing the grave. We spend our time, money, and energy to project the appearance that death has no hold on us. But there is a better way. When Paul was writing to Christian believers in Rome, he was writing to people who lived in a precarious age when Christians were being persecuted—some even losing their lives because of what they believed. And to these believers, who were so very much like you or me, he offered another way of seeing, another way of *being*. "Whether we live or die," he exhorted them, "we belong to the Lord." You and I do as well. Whatever you are facing that scares you, have confidence in what matters most: you belong to God.

God, You know my heart. You know the fears of which I'm aware and the ones that drive me in ways I can't even see. And yet in life and in death, I belong to You. Amen.

Trust in the Lord Forever

Open the gates that the righteous nation may enter, the nation that keeps faith. You will keep in perfect peace those whose minds are steadfast, because they trust in you. Trust in the LORD forever, for the LORD, the LORD himself, is the Rock eternal.

ISAIAH 26:2–4

When Christians who live privileged lives travel to be among believers in cultures that aren't as affluent, where people face the sting of poverty daily, these affluent Christians are often surprised and transformed by the experience. They are blessed as they witness firsthand the satisfaction that is possible for those who have truly found their security and joy in God and not in their human circumstances. Frankly, it can be a little baffling for those of us raised to believe that *we* are the ones who are "blessed" because of our abundance. But this reality is the melody that dances throughout the holy scriptures. God assures us that we experience peace as we set our minds and hearts on God. Our satisfaction has less to do with our circumstances and more to do with the One in whom we put our trust. When we trust the One who is called the eternal Rock, we experience life that really is life.

Father, I confess that I have sought my security in that which is not You. But my heart yearns to be grounded, solid, secure as I put my trust in You. Quicken my heart today to remember that You are my Rock. Amen.

God Has a Plan for You

And we know that in all things God works for the good of those who love him, who have been called according to his purpose. For those God foreknew he also predestined to be conformed to the image of his Son, that he might be the firstborn among many brothers and sisters.

ROMANS 8:28–29

Our lives don't always look the way we thought they might look, do they? Maybe you're looking and hoping for romantic love. Or perhaps you're struggling financially right now. Or during this season you might be facing an unexpected health issue. The hardships we face can narrow our vision to the situation, the struggle, the pain that is most palpable in our daily lives. But in his letter to the Romans, Paul gives us a much bigger picture of God's good plan for our lives. He assures us that in ways we can't fully see or comprehend, God works behind the scenes for our good in all things. And Paul traces the bigger story for our lives as those who were always meant to belong to God—to discover our identities in Him and to live lives that look like Jesus' life. If the troubles in your life today have made your vision *small*, lift your eyes to your Maker and ask Him to show you a bigger picture.

God, open my eyes to the bigger story of which I am a part. Today, despite what I am facing, I purpose to find my life in You. Amen.

Set Your Mind on Things Above

Since, then, you have been raised with Christ, set your hearts on things above, where Christ is, seated at the right hand of God. Set your minds on things above, not on earthly things. For you died, and your life is now hidden with Christ in God.

COLOSSIANS 3:1–3

Whether it's scribbled on a scrap of paper or typed into a note on your phone, I wonder if your list of things to get done looks anything like the lists of the women I know. Though the particulars vary, the tasks are predictable: go to the grocery store; buy a birthday gift; prepare for tomorrow's presentation at work; send a check; pick up dry cleaning; do the laundry; return neighbor's casserole dish; prep for book club. . .and the list goes on. When so much is pressing on us, our minds can feel scattered, and we can feel undone. But in his letter to folks who were a lot like us, Paul offers a reminder to set our minds on things above. And while that can almost feel like one more thing to put on the list, it's the best way to stay grounded in what is most real and most true.

God, You know that my life is full and that I struggle to keep my mind stayed on Christ. Be my helper today. Send Your Spirit into my heart and mind so that my heart stays fixed on You. Amen.

When You Call, God Answers

"This is what the Lord *says, he who made the earth, the* Lord *who formed it and established it—the* Lord *is his name: 'Call to me and I will answer you and tell you great and unsearchable things you do not know.' "*

Jeremiah 33:2–3

For some of us, our days feel as though they're filled with communications we hope evoke a response. We phone a sibling. We message a doctor. We email a client. We voice text a friend. And if we're feeling really crazy, we might even walk down the block and knock on a neighbor's door to have a real conversation. But phone calls go unreturned. Messages wait unanswered. And finding a friend at home can be hit or miss. Our hearts yearn to be heard and addressed, but sometimes we encounter only disappointing silence. But through the prophet Jeremiah, we hear a voice that beckons us, "Call to me and I will answer you and tell you great and unsearchable things you do not know." When we seek God—the One who made heaven and earth!—God is faithful to answer. Sometimes God answers through scripture. Other times we may hear God speaking through a friend. And sometimes we experience a still, small knowing as God's Spirit communicates to our hearts. Beloved, when you speak to God, God hears and answers.

Lord, I trust the promise of Your Word assuring me that when I speak, You hear. And when You hear, You answer. Thank You for this sacred assurance. Amen.

Wash One Another's Feet

"Now that I, your Lord and Teacher, have washed your feet, you also should wash one another's feet. I have set you an example that you should do as I have done for you. . . . Now that you know these things, you will be blessed if you do them."

JOHN 13:14–15, 17

Back in the day, the job of foot washing was reserved for lowly servants. So when Jesus stooped over to wash Peter's dirty feet, Peter resisted. But Jesus, who was modeling how His followers were to live, insisted on washing His friend's feet. And Jesus coached His friends to do for one another what He had done for them. What will "foot washing" look like in your life? Maybe it will mean scrubbing a friend's feet before a mani-pedi, but it also might mean serving her in other ways: listening to her when she's having a rough day, treating her to lunch, or showing up at her house after a family member dies. Ask God how you are being called to serve your friends in His name.

Jesus, thank You for showing us the best way to live. Inspire and equip me today to live a life of love for others the way that You did. Amen.

Do Not Fear

But now, this is what the LORD says—he who created you, Jacob, he who formed you, Israel: "Do not fear, for I have redeemed you; I have summoned you by name; you are mine. When you pass through the waters, I will be with you; and when you pass through the rivers, they will not sweep over you. When you walk through the fire, you will not be burned; the flames will not set you ablaze."

ISAIAH 43:1–2

Daily we are triggered to fear. The news reports a shooting that happened too close to home. A routine lab test shows troubling results. A friend's marriage comes undone. A person we love continues to make dangerous choices. Sometimes consciously and sometimes unconsciously, we carry this fear in our bodies, our hearts, our minds. We try to be brave, but our help isn't a matter of us mustering our own courage. Our *help* is in the name of the Lord. Beloved, when you feel afraid, listen again and again to the voice of the One who says, "You are mine." And when you can hear that voice and see that voice, hear the assurance of the One who loves you: "I will be with you." God's sure presence with us, in the waters and the fires, is our reliable comfort.

Lord, You know the deep concerns and fears of my heart. Today I take my eyes off You, and I look to Your face. I listen for Your voice. I am not afraid because You are near. Amen.

You Are My Light

"You are the salt of the earth. But if the salt loses its saltiness, how can it be made salty again? It is no longer good for anything, except to be thrown out and trampled underfoot. You are the light of the world. A town built on a hill cannot be hidden. Neither do people light a lamp and put it under a bowl. Instead they put it on its stand, and it gives light to everyone in the house. In the same way, let your light shine before others, that they may see your good deeds and glorify your Father in heaven."

Matthew 5:13–16

In the ancient world, the role of being a bearer of light, "the light of the world," was assigned to kings. So when Jesus announces to a crowd that had gathered to hear Him preach, "You are the light of the world," they would have been blown away by the audacious claim! And they should have been because it was pretty bold for an itinerant teacher to tell humble farmers and potters and carpenters that *they* were the light of the world. That's huge! Sister, God has called you worthy of bearing His light to the world. And Jesus is inviting you to shine your light so that others may glorify your Father.

Though I feel humbled by the assignment, Father, help me to shine today. By the power of Your Spirit, may the light of Your glory touch the lives of those around me, in Jesus' name. Amen.

Ways Higher Than Mine

Seek the Lord while he may be found; call on him while he is near. Let the wicked forsake their ways and the unrighteous their thoughts. Let them turn to the Lord, and he will have mercy on them, and to our God, for he will freely pardon. "For my thoughts are not your thoughts, neither are your ways my ways," declares the Lord. "As the heavens are higher than the earth, so are my ways higher than your ways and my thoughts than your thoughts."

Isaiah 55:6–9

After Jane's marriage ended, she was single for over a decade. During that season, she longed to find a life partner. But after twelve long years, Jane met a man who loved her the way Christ loved her. Until that moment, if you'd asked Jane the reason she was still single longer than she would have chosen, she couldn't have told you. She didn't understand why she was alone. Some of us face financial hardships we wouldn't have chosen. Or disease. Or the death of loved ones. We don't understand God's ways. Isaiah exhorts, "My thoughts are not your thoughts, neither are your ways my ways." Today as you pray, quiet your heart and offer God the parts of your life that don't make sense, and seek His ways.

God, although I don't understand, I put my trust in You.
I offer You what I don't yet understand, trusting in
Your mercy, Your love, and Your kindness. Amen.

Fed by More Than Bread

Jesus, full of the Holy Spirit, left the Jordan and was led by the Spirit into the wilderness, where for forty days he was tempted by the devil. He ate nothing during those days, and at the end of them he was hungry. The devil said to him, "If you are the Son of God, tell this stone to become bread." Jesus answered, "It is written: 'Man shall not live on bread alone.' "

Luke 4:1–4

When we read about Jesus' temptation in the wilderness, it's natural to deduce that the test Jesus faced was fasting for forty days. But pastor and author Eugene Peterson reminds us that those forty days of prayer and fasting were actually just *preparation* for the real test! And when the devil comes to Jesus, He is ready. And because the enemy twists what is true, he appeals to Jesus' Sonship when he asks Him to perform a miracle of which he knows Jesus is capable. Faithful, Jesus refuses, citing scripture: "Man shall not live on bread alone." Though He is hungry and weary, Jesus is fueled by something bigger than carbs in that moment! When we are tempted, God feeds us with His presence. He nourishes us with scripture. The Lord provides all we need when we trust in Him.

Father of Jesus and Father of mine, I seek my sustenance in You today. Fortify me to resist false substitutes, and feed with what truly satisfies. Amen.

God Notices the Weak

"Blessed are the poor in spirit, for theirs is the kingdom of heaven. Blessed are those who mourn, for they will be comforted. Blessed are the meek, for they will inherit the earth. Blessed are those who hunger and thirst for righteousness, for they will be filled."

MATTHEW 5:3–6

The values of people and cultures in the ancient world weren't so different from what our world esteems today. People noticed and esteemed those who were proud and confident. They cheered those who had all wins and no losses. They respected those who could boast of achievements. They revered those who pursued success. Whether it was a next-door neighbor or the king of a neighboring nation, the human impulse to strive to be self-sufficient was the same as it is today. And yet Jesus turns this natural human impulse on its head. He surprises His listeners and probably disappoints those who were hoping He'd *be* a mighty king when He teaches that God's values turn the world's priorities upside down. What was bad news for the rich and powerful was good news for the poor and marginalized. What they were learning from Jesus was revolutionary: the poor in spirit, those who grieve, those who are meek, and those whose biggest desire is to be righteous before God are the ones who *win*.

Lord, transform my heart and mind so that I value what You value. Remind me that in my weakness, I find my value in You. Shape me into a person whose satisfaction is belonging to You. Amen.

God's Strategy to Defeat Your Enemies

If your enemy is hungry, give him food to eat; if he is thirsty, give him water to drink. In doing this, you will heap burning coals on his head, and the Lord will reward you.

Proverbs 25:21–22

After an unpleasant encounter, a teenage girl leaves a kind note in the locker of the girl who bullies her daily at school. Before she goes to work, a woman who has been unjustly accused by a work colleague prays for her accuser daily. When it is raining at the bus stop, a college student offers a ride to the young woman who beat her out for the last spot on the debate team. Although our natural temptation is to rage at our enemies, to despise them, to malign them, or to hurt them, God leads us to love our enemies in surprising ways. And although we can be tempted to believe that caring for our enemies is "weak," scripture names it as one of the mightiest weapons at our disposal! We honor God—and we even experience satisfaction—when we answer evil with good. What is the situation in your life today where you are being called to love your enemy in a radical way?

God, I confess that I would rather hurt my enemy than help her. I'd rather blame him than bless him. By Your Spirit, though, empower me to bless my enemy today. Amen.

You Need Not Carry All Your Fears

Humble yourselves, therefore, under God's mighty hand, that he may lift you up in due time. Cast all your anxiety on him because he cares for you.
1 Peter 5:6–7

The moment she woke up, Lisa felt heavy. She dreaded the mountain of work that waited for her at the office. She worried about the dangerous choices her teenage son had been making. She'd been putting off scheduling an appointment with her doctor, but she knew it was time. And she felt anxious about a tricky situation that was unfolding at church. Flooded by these concerns, she struggled to find the energy to haul herself out of bed. But when she paused to open her daily devotional, she read an affirmation from God's Word that reoriented her for the day: "Cast all your anxiety on him because he cares for you." She was reminded that she didn't have to carry that heavy load. Prayerfully, one by one, she released her burdens into God's care. At the end of the day, before her head hit the pillow, she did the same thing! Beloved, God receives all your anxieties because He cares for *you*.

God, I thank You that You care for me. And I offer You the concerns that weigh on my heart today. They are too heavy for me, and I believe that You receive them from me and carry them for me. Amen.

This Is Your Mission

The Lord is my shepherd, I lack nothing.
Psalm 23:1

Have you ever browsed through Ted Talks online? The purpose of this series of presentations is that each speaker shares one *big idea* that can change the lives of the people in the audience. Maybe a speaker who's been bullied inspires kindness in the audience. Or maybe a presenter who has a disability helps the audience to view disability in a new way. Or perhaps a billionaire offers the single secret to becoming wealthy! The big idea is meant to be life changing for the listener. In arguably the most popular psalm in the book's collection of 150 writings, the author declares that because God is his caregiver, he wants for nothing. And although it might have slipped right past you as you were memorizing Psalm 23 in third grade, this is one big life-changing idea! Because God is *your* shepherd, you lack nothing. The ancient truth actually resonates with recent discoveries that people who practice gratitude are the people who are most satisfied. Beloved, because the Lord is your shepherd, there's nothing more you need. Soak in that life-changing reality today.

Father, You have made Yourself known as the Shepherd who is good, and I believe that You are faithful to provide all I need. Today and each day, I choose to remain grounded in that transforming reality. Amen.

The Way to Get Dressed Each Morning

Therefore, as God's chosen people, holy and dearly loved, clothe yourselves with compassion, kindness, humility, gentleness and patience. Bear with each other and forgive one another if any of you has a grievance against someone. Forgive as the Lord forgave you. And over all these virtues put on love, which binds them all together in perfect unity.

COLOSSIANS 3:12–14

Scrambling to get out the door on time, you hurry through your morning routine: pulling on your shirt, buttoning your pants, smoothing your socks, tying your shoes, throwing on a coat. You dress so that you are prepared for the day. And in his letter to the church at Colossae, Paul exhorts the believers to clothe themselves with what prepares them to be God's people in the world. Today, before you leave home, slip on compassion. Wear kindness. Don humility. Pull on gentleness. Slide into patience. Wear forgiveness. And as you're dashing toward the door, reach into the closet and grab *love*. Put love on over all these things. If you're in a real hurry and only have time to grab one, choose to put on *love*. Love is what you need to live as God's chosen daughter, holy and beloved.

Lord, without the clothing You provide, I am vulnerable and weak. Clothe me with Your character today so that I might love others in Your name. Amen.

Choices That Lead to Life

Blessed is the one who does not walk in step with the wicked or stand in the way that sinners take or sit in the company of mockers, but whose delight is in the law of the Lord, and who meditates on his law day and night. That person is like a tree planted by streams of water, which yields its fruit in season and whose leaf does not wither—whatever they do prospers.

Psalm 1:1–3

When a teenager starts making poor choices and getting into trouble, her parents are quick to look at the company she keeps. Is she spending time with those who are getting into trouble, or is she choosing to be with friends who inspire her to do her best? The collection of psalms in the Bible *begins* with the kind of commonsense wisdom that teaches us what we can do to prosper. Avoid the wicked. Delight in God's law. Hold it in your heart. When you do that, you're like a strong tree that bears fruit. As you notice the fabric of your life right now, are you making choices that will help you to thrive? Do you avoid what is wicked? Do you delight in God's Word? Do you find ways to hold it in your heart? Beloved, you were made to flourish, and God is showing you the way to do it.

Lord, I long to flourish and to yield fruit for You.
Open my eyes to the ways I've failed to choose the good way, and lead me in the way that leads to life. Amen.

God Has Spoken to You

In the past God spoke to our ancestors through the prophets at many times and in various ways, but in these last days he has spoken to us by his Son, whom he appointed heir of all things, and through whom also he made the universe. The Son is the radiance of God's glory and the exact representation of his being, sustaining all things by his powerful word.

Hebrews 1:1–3

I have a friend who hears God speak to her in ways that she understands. Sometimes she hears an audible voice, and other times she describes perceiving God's leading in her spirit. I confess that it can be tempting to envy her this intelligible communication. Although it's not quite as Hollywood glamorous as the audible voice, God does speak clearly to us through His Word. The author of Hebrews reminds us that God spoke to our ancestors through the voices of the prophets, and today God speaks to His people through His Son. Jesus carries on the tradition of the prophets by serving as a mouthpiece for God. And graciously, you and I can listen to God through the Jesus we meet in scripture. We can hear God speaking clearly as we encounter the living Christ through His holy Word.

Speak, Lord, for Your servant is listening. Father, I am confident that I can hear Your voice speaking clearly through the person of Jesus. Speak to the ears of my heart today, in Jesus' name, amen.

Hearing and Doing the Word

Do not merely listen to the word, and so deceive yourselves. Do what it says. Anyone who listens to the word but does not do what it says is like someone who looks at his face in a mirror and, after looking at himself, goes away and immediately forgets what he looks like. But whoever looks intently into the perfect law that gives freedom, and continues in it—not forgetting what they have heard, but doing it—they will be blessed in what they do.

James 1:22–25

Let's say that a good friend gave you a fabulous cookbook for your birthday, and it was compiled by a world-famous chef. Before you went to bed that night, you opened it and pored over dozens of fabulous recipes. The next morning, you reached for it on your nightstand to read it before you even got out of bed. Day after day you studied the recipes, even committing some to memory. But after several months, you still hadn't attempted to cook any of them! That would be crazy, right? James warns that we can be tempted to hear God's Word but not obey it. And when we do, when we gobble it up without ever responding in faithful obedience, we deceive ourselves. Beloved, purpose today both to be nourished by God's Word and to respond by living it out. It's what we're made for.

Lord, I am Yours. I have heard You speaking clearly through Your Word, and I long to live in response to Your voice. Guide my steps today as I follow You. Amen.

He Suffered Because He Loves You

Surely he took up our pain and bore our suffering, yet we considered him punished by God, stricken by him, and afflicted. But he was pierced for our transgressions, he was crushed for our iniquities; the punishment that brought us peace was on him, and by his wounds we are healed. We all, like sheep, have gone astray, each of us has turned to our own way; and the LORD has laid on him the iniquity of us all.

ISAIAH 53:4–6

One of the tricky ways the enemy undermines a life of loving relationship with God is by hinting to us that our salvation is incomplete. When we sin, he hisses that we are unforgivably guilty. When we struggle, he insists we're not worthy of grace. When we are lonely, he suggests that God doesn't really care for us. But the prophet Isaiah foretold a very different story. Through Isaiah, God promised a suffering servant who would take our punishment upon Himself. Even when we stumble, the victory Jesus achieved on the cross is *complete*. It is finished, and we can depend on it. So the next time you recognize the lying voice of the accuser, return to this passage in Isaiah. Speak it out loud to thwart the schemes of the deceiver.

Jesus, thank You for Your work on the cross. In You, I am forgiven once and for all. Today I reject the lying voice of the enemy, and I claim the true word of Your salvation. Amen.

Seeing Is Believing

Jesus performed many other signs in the presence of his disciples, which are not recorded in this book. But these are written that you may believe that Jesus is the Messiah, the Son of God, and that by believing you may have life in his name.

John 20:30–31

Someone who claims to be your friend gossips about you with others. You've scheduled a phone call with a potential client, but they never call or let you know why. A child promises to do his or her chores, but days go by and they remain undone. You don't need to be convinced that a person's actions speak louder than their words. What they say isn't as important as what they do, because what we can observe—or what we're shown—is much more persuasive than what we're told. Those around Jesus saw the miracles He performed with their eyes: feeding the hungry, healing the sick, blessing the poor. And scripture has captured many of those so that we too might see, hear, believe, and have life in His name. As you read the Gospels, God is revealed as you witness the actions of Jesus.

Lord, open my eyes to see Your face and hear Your voice. Continue to show me who You are through the miracles I see Jesus perform. Thank You for Your Word that allows me to know You and find life in You. Amen.

Filled with God's Power

But we have this treasure in jars of clay to show that this all-surpassing power is from God and not from us. We are hard pressed on every side, but not crushed; perplexed, but not in despair; persecuted, but not abandoned; struck down, but not destroyed.

2 Corinthians 4:7–9

After a lump of clay has been formed into a jar, it is fired in a blazing-hot kiln. The firing process strengthens the jar, but it's still vulnerable to cracks. When the jar is cracked, its contents leak out. Coffee, tea, or soup seep out of the cracks and crevices. Paul writes to the church in Corinth that we carry the beautiful gift of God we've been given as if in clay jars, so that it might be clear that the treasure is God's and not our own. Paul acknowledges that although we're pressed, perplexed, persecuted, and struck down, we are filled with the power of God! And as vessels of God's grace, it is His power at work in us and through us to bless the world He loves. So, as lives are touched and transformed by God's grace, it is clear that God is the One at work and not us.

God, take my weakness and use it for building up Your kingdom. Where I am weak, may Your glory shine most brightly. Amen.

God's Ways Are Not Our Ways

But Joseph said to them, "Don't be afraid. Am I in the place of God? You intended to harm me, but God intended it for good to accomplish what is now being done, the saving of many lives. So then, don't be afraid. I will provide for you and your children." And he reassured them and spoke kindly to them.

GENESIS 50:19–21

Ellen, a precious friend of mine, has faced more than her fair share of suffering. She has lost a child, suffered through her husband's infidelities, weathered divorce, and now faces a degenerative disease. Some would equate her to a female version of Job! But the wisdom and courage she's demonstrated are more reminiscent of Joseph. The man who was kidnapped and sold into slavery by his brothers, wrongfully accused, and thrown into prison understood that God had a bigger plan for his life than his circumstances would suggest. What his brothers intended for harm, God intended for good, redeeming Joseph's circumstances for His glory. I've seen the same thing in Ellen's life. Because of her steadfast faithfulness to God, so much good has come out of her circumstances. Like Joseph, she has been blessed and has been a blessing to others.

Lord, I confess that I don't understand all of what I'm facing in my life right now. It's hard for me to see how it can be used for good. But I put my faith in You and trust that You are a mighty Redeemer. Amen.

Where There Is No More Death

And I heard a loud voice from the throne saying, "Look! God's dwelling place is now among the people, and he will dwell with them. They will be his people, and God himself will be with them and be their God. 'He will wipe every tear from their eyes. There will be no more death' or mourning or crying or pain, for the old order of things has passed away."

REVELATION 21:3–4

Right now we're living in broken bodies with broken hearts in a broken world. Children are shot by stray bullets. Teenagers succumb to cancer. Marriages end. Illness wreaks havoc in lives and families. And you know the ways that sin and death have impacted your life. All around us, it appears as though death is winning. But we know the rest of the story, don't we? We know that the One who died and rose from the grave has conquered the power of sin and death in the world and in our lives. And because of Jesus' work on the cross, we have the assurance that when we are with God, death will have been defeated. In heaven, where the old order will have passed away, there will be no more tears. Thanks be to God!

Lord, I believe that You have already achieved victory over sin and death. And I know that when I am at last with You, I will no longer experience mourning, crying, or pain. Ignite the hope of glory in my heart as I wait for the promise of eternity with You. Amen.

You Were My God Before I Was Born

Yet you brought me out of the womb; you made me trust in you, even at my mother's breast. From birth I was cast on you; from my mother's womb you have been my God.
PSALM 22:9–10

Some of us measure our life with God from the date we were water baptized. Others of us name our new birth as the day when we accepted the Gospel of Jesus Christ. Others point to a moment of being baptized in the Holy Spirit. But the psalmist recognizes God's gracious presence from before he could *choose* for God. The writer recognizes God's loving hand as the one bringing him out of the womb and even upon the babe suckling at a mother's breast. It is a beautiful picture of complete dependence on God. This week, as you pause to be still with God, prayerfully imagine your own beginnings. Whether your arrival into the world was celebrated or not, invite God to show you those earliest moments of your life. Close your eyes and see God being fully present with you as you entered the world.

God, I praise You that I belong to You. You brought me from my mother's womb, and You held me in my earliest days. Lord, I thank You that I belong to You and that my worth comes from that belonging. Amen.

You Know the Sound of His Voice

"When he has brought out all his own, he goes on ahead of them, and his sheep follow him because they know his voice. But they will never follow a stranger; in fact, they will run away from him because they do not recognize a stranger's voice."

John 10:4–5

Maybe you were a child playing outside after dark, and you heard your mother call for you to come home. Or perhaps as an adult you were in a crowd and recognized the voice of your best friend. Our ears are alert to the sound of the voice we know and trust. But when a telemarketer calls and butchers your name? Or an online scam artist messages you and calls you the wrong name? You know not to blindly follow the voice you do not recognize. Jesus says that the sheep who know Him follow the sound of His voice. We learn to discern His voice as we spend time with Him and as we overhear Him leading others. When we're in the presence of Jesus, in prayer and in scripture, we learn to recognize the voice of our Shepherd.

Jesus, the Good Shepherd, thank You for all the ways You lead and care for me. You feed me, You protect me, and You offer me rest. Today when I hear Your voice, empower me to respond in obedience to You. Amen.

Slow to Anger and Rich in Love

The Lord is gracious and compassionate, slow to anger and rich in love. The Lord is good to all; he has compassion on all he has made. All your works praise you, Lord; your faithful people extol you.
Psalm 145:8–10

When people are invited to imagine God, some picture an angry judge in a black robe, slamming a gavel and announcing, "Guilty!" Others see a stern police officer monitoring their behavior. And still others hear the hard religious words of an angry preacher who is chronically disappointed in their behavior. And yet the God of the Bible is actually identified as one who is *slow* to anger—who is rich in love. This benevolent God is one who is gracious and compassionate. Can you picture a divine countenance that is gracious and kind? Can you see a face that is compassionate and merciful? Beloved, the Lord longs to be gracious to you. As you pray this week, notice what face you have given to God. If it is one that is angry, disappointed, and judgmental, offer that image to God with open hands. And ask the Lord to replace that distorted image with a face that reflects both your worth and His abundant kindness.

God, when I see You, I often see a distorted picture of who You really are. Open my eyes to recognize You. By Your Spirit, help me to see Your face, which is gracious and kind. Amen.

Keeping a Tight Rein on Your Tongue

Those who consider themselves religious and yet do not keep a tight rein on their tongues deceive themselves, and their religion is worthless.
James 1:26

During Jesus' earthly ministry, He surprised a lot of people. So much of what He preached, taught, and lived turned conventional religion on its head. He wanted all to know that the kingdom of God He was ushering in was different from anything they knew or expected. "*You thought you had to offer sacrifices? Surprise! I've brought grace. You thought you had to do all the right religious things? Surprise! God actually cares about your heart and mind and lips!*" Because James had spent so much time with Jesus, he was one of Jesus' followers who continued to echo Jesus' teachings after His resurrection and ascension. James wanted to make sure believers understood that their religion wasn't worth much if their tongues—an expression of what's in their hearts—weren't glorifying God.

How does James's admonition speak to your heart today? Are there ways that God is calling you to build others up with your words rather than tear them down? Is God calling you to encourage, inspire, and bless others with your tongue? Ask God today to show you how to honor Him with your speech.

Lord, I long to glorify You in all I do. Open my ears to hear how the words I speak celebrate or degrade others. Teach me to honor the image of God that You have imprinted upon every person You have made. Amen.

Your Maker Neither Slumbers nor Sleeps

I lift up my eyes to the mountains—where does my help come from? My help comes from the LORD, the Maker of heaven and earth. He will not let your foot slip—he who watches over you will not slumber; indeed, he who watches over Israel will neither slumber nor sleep.

PSALM 121:1–4

A lot of us wrestle with anxiety. We worry that we've said or done the wrong thing. We're concerned about the details of our lives that we can't control. We're anxious about what will happen tomorrow, and next week, and next year. And we're tempted to seek comfort wherever it can be found: eating, shopping, drinking, or exercising. But the psalmist has found a better way and welcomes us into it. The writer reminds us that the One who watches over us—the One who is present and alert to carry our burdens and concerns—never falls asleep on the job. As you notice anxieties rise in your heart, close your eyes and visualize yourself handing them over to the One who cares. No matter what you're carrying, God is ready and willing to receive the burdens and anxieties you're holding.

God, the cares and anxieties I carry are too heavy for me, and so I offer You the concerns of my heart. Confident that You are the One from whom my help comes, I release them to You. Amen.

Practicing Hospitality

Be joyful in hope, patient in affliction, faithful in prayer. Share with the Lord's people who are in need. Practice hospitality.

Romans 12:12–13

After a long, hard day at work or caring for family members, it can be tempting to drive into a parking space or garage, shut the door, hole up at home, and live a life that's pretty isolated. Too often we're not only isolated from our own neighbors, we're separated even farther from those who are most vulnerable. Naturally preferring comfort over discomfort, we distance ourselves from a world in need.

But Paul invites followers of Jesus to pursue real life by living differently. Not only are we called not to avoid folks in need, we're actually commissioned to pursue them, meeting their needs and welcoming them into our homes. Maybe you'll invite a widow from church to join you for brunch. Perhaps you'll welcome the kids of a single mom for a weekend sleepover. Or maybe you'll invite a neighbor to dinner whom you've never met. As a believer, you were created to share the beautiful life of Jesus with those around you.

Father, just as You have called me worthy, You have also bestowed inestimable worth on those around me who are in need. Open my eyes to see those whom You are calling me to welcome in Your name. I offer myself to You as an instrument of Your grace. Amen.

You Were Made for Freedom

It is for freedom that Christ has set us free. Stand firm, then, and do not let yourselves be burdened again by a yoke of slavery.
GALATIANS 5:1

Our culture has convinced a lot of us that we deserve to be happy. We deserve to be satisfied. We deserve pleasure. Many of us have believed the subtle lie that we are *free* to do whatever makes us feel good. And yet when we pursue what we think will make us happy—buying too much, owning too much, eating too much, drinking too much—we end up enslaved to what once promised to make us happy! We're crushed by credit card bills. Our physical health declines. Our relationships suffer. Paul reminds us that we have been set free to live authentic, abundant life. So, he invites us to stand firm and reject a yoke of slavery when we've already been set free. Is there a way that you've sacrificed your freedom in Christ? Ask the Spirit to show you where you are bound, and *choose* freedom.

Jesus, Redeemer, thank You for setting me free by Your work on the cross! If there are ways I've submitted again to a yoke of slavery, open my eyes so that I might choose freedom in You. Strengthen me, by the power of Your Spirit, to live into the freedom You offer. Amen.

Love from Everlasting to Everlasting

But from everlasting to everlasting the Lord's love is with those who fear him, and his righteousness with their children's children—with those who keep his covenant and remember to obey his precepts.

Psalm 103:17–18

Almost every woman I know has experienced a rupture in a significant relationship in her life. One lost a parent to death when she was a teen. One endured a difficult marriage to a husband who was unfaithful. Another lost a young adult child to death. And another suffered as a result of a loved one's addiction. But scripture promises that there is One who can love us fully and perfectly. In some places the Bible refers to God as a loving and gracious Father. And in other places, God is revealed as a faithful husband to an unfaithful bride. The steadfast, faithful love of the Lord that we see showered onto people just like us in the Bible stands above human love. The hurts we've endured in human relationships are noticed, touched, and transformed by the One whose love is from everlasting to everlasting. Beloved, you are worthy of this perfect love.

God, You know the hurts of my heart. You know where I've been wounded in my relationships with others, and You long to redeem. Today I open my heart to receive Your love that does not fail. Amen.

Worth Far More Than You Can Imagine

"Are not five sparrows sold for two pennies? Yet not one of them is forgotten by God. Indeed, the very hairs of your head are all numbered. Don't be afraid; you are worth more than many sparrows."

LUKE 12:6–7

Having a robust and healthy sense of self-esteem is a relatively modern concept. The biblical writers were more concerned about naming and communicating the identity of a community than that of an individual. And yet when Jesus was teaching the masses, most of whom were poor, hungry, and struggling, He wanted each one to know how very precious he or she was to God. So, He taught them by speaking about something relatively cheap and without value in the culture: sparrows. He essentially says, "They're cheap, and you consider them worthless, but God is aware of each little bird." And the care that God has for this seemingly insignificant creature, Jesus continues, is nothing compared to the care God has for you. In fact, God knows you so intimately and cares for you so deeply that He actually knows how many hairs are on your head! "You," Jesus promises His audience and assures you and me, "are worth more than many sparrows."

Father, I admit that it's hard for me to wrap my mind around Your love for me. But in Jesus' words I do hear that You see me, You know me, and You love me. God, today I will rest in the assurance that You care for me. Amen.

A Compassionate God Sees Your Suffering

"If you take your neighbor's cloak as a pledge, return it by sunset, because that cloak is the only covering your neighbor has. What else can they sleep in? When they cry out to me, I will hear, for I am compassionate."

Exodus 22:26–27

In the five Old Testament books called the Pentateuch, God gives His people the law. The law is meant to guide and protect them. If they follow it, God assures them they will live long and prosper. One of these rules of conduct God establishes is to return any cloak that one has borrowed by sunset so that the one who lent it doesn't get cold at night. While the ancient rule feels, in some ways, like common courtesy, it is driven by God's fierce love for those who are vulnerable. When those who are weak, poor, or vulnerable cry out to God, He hears their cry.

And what was true for an ancient people is true for you and me today. The same God of compassion hears us, sees us, and loves us. When we cry out to God, God hears. Whether it's a concern at home, a situation at work, a financial worry, or a health prognosis, God hears the cries of your heart. Be bold this week in crying out to God to meet your deep needs.

Lord, I thank You that You are a God of compassion. You know the ways I am vulnerable. You know what I need, and You care. Thank You for Your loving attention to my heart and to my situation. Amen.

Jesus Loves You as He Is Loved

"Righteous Father, though the world does not know you, I know you, and they know that you have sent me. I have made you known to them, and will continue to make you known in order that the love you have for me may be in them and that I myself may be in them."

John 17:25–26

Advertisers grab our attention by convincing us that a particular purchase will guarantee us remarkable results. Whether it's the fuel that won the race or the cereal that got an athlete across the finish line, promoters want us to believe that we can see similar results if we're fueled by the *same* stuff. At the end of His earthly ministry, we hear Jesus praying to His Father, assuring Him that He's carried out His assignment. Jesus promises to continue to make the Father known so that the love the Father has for Jesus may be in the ones Jesus loves. That's you! And me! Don't miss what Jesus is saying. The very same love that the Father has for Jesus, Jesus has for us. And Jesus Himself promises to live in us as well. Take some time this week to soak in this truth. The big love God has for the Son is the same love that Jesus has for us.

Jesus, thank You that I can listen in on Your conversation with Your Father and mine! And thank You for Your abundant love for me. Help me to receive the fullness of Your grace in my deep places that I might be rooted and grounded in Your love. Amen.

God Heals the Brokenhearted

The Lord builds up Jerusalem; he gathers the exiles of Israel. He heals the brokenhearted and binds up their wounds. He determines the number of the stars and calls them each by name.
Psalm 147:2–4

Throughout scripture, God's people have known what it is to live in exile. Adam and Eve were evicted from the garden. Abraham was sent from his homeland to the land God would provide. Moses spent his whole life in exile. A modern equivalent to exiles might be those who flee their homeland due to violence to live in foreign lands. Even if they carve out a life for themselves, a part of them that has lost home is left brokenhearted. Graciously, the God of Israel is One who is attentive to those with broken hearts. He takes notice and binds up their wounds. Beloved, today God knows the ways that you are brokenhearted. You may not have lost your home, but you may have suffered other losses. The Lord sees. The Lord knows. The Lord cares. God is attentive to hurting hearts and longs to heal and bind up the brokenhearted. Because He is reliable, offer God the hurts of your heart today.

Lord, I thank You that You care about me. You notice the ways my heart has been bruised, and You bend down to bind it up. I ask for Your healing and trust that You are the Great Physician who cares for me. Amen.

Jesus Wants to Be with You

He wanted to see who Jesus was, but because he was short he could not see over the crowd. So he ran ahead and climbed a sycamore-fig tree to see him, since Jesus was coming that way. When Jesus reached the spot, he looked up and said to him, "Zacchaeus, come down immediately. I must stay at your house today." So he came down at once and welcomed him gladly.

Luke 19:3–6

The scene Luke describes of Jesus' encounter with a man named Zacchaeus is a beautiful, holy glimpse into who Jesus is. Zacchaeus was a tax collector—a job that should *not* be equated with an IRS agent. No, in the first century, tax collectors were known to exploit the people from whom they were assigned to collect taxes, demanding more money than was owed so that they could skim off the top for themselves. Zacchaeus would have been despised in his community. Yet in a crowd of people who'd gathered to see Jesus—something like a modern parade down Main Street USA—Jesus saw Zacchaeus, welcomed him to come closer, and invited Himself to Zacchaeus's home. The radical act wasn't lost on the crowd. In witnessing Jesus' graciousness toward one they deemed undeserving, the crowds discovered firsthand that the most unlikely among us is *worthy*.

Jesus, grant me Your vision to see the inherent worth of every individual You have created. And teach me to love like You love. Amen.

God Has Good in Store for You

You prepare a table before me in the presence of my enemies. You anoint my head with oil; my cup overflows. Surely your goodness and love will follow me all the days of my life, and I will dwell in the house of the LORD forever.

PSALM 23:5–6

When we experience bad things, we wonder whether God has good in store for us. If we suffer the loss of a job, we wonder whether God is a good provider. When others seem to prosper and flourish while we flounder, we wonder if God cares for us. When our relationships are broken, we question whether God is at the helm. But the psalmist who has experienced the tender care of a good Shepherd introduces us to a God who cares for us. The One who loves you, feeds you, and blesses you in abundance! He watches over you, eager to meet all your needs. Beloved, God's love is with you today. Choose to dwell in the reality of that love.

Lord, I confess that when life gets hard, I wonder whether You are in my corner. Today I celebrate and praise You as the One who provides for all my needs. Open my eyes to see the many ways You are blessing me today. Thank You for Your steadfast, faithful care. Amen.

God's Spirit Is at Work, Making You New

And do not grieve the Holy Spirit of God, with whom you were sealed for the day of redemption. Get rid of all bitterness, rage and anger, brawling and slander, along with every form of malice. Be kind and compassionate to one another, forgiving each other, just as in Christ God forgave you.

EPHESIANS 4:30–32

When our lives were claimed by Christ, we became new creatures. Invigorated by new life, we may have noticed fresh growth and transformation in our lives. But as months or years passed, some of our old habits may have crept back in. Old behaviors that had been put to death reappear, and some days we wonder whether our lives are any different from what they once were. But God's Spirit is still at work in our hearts and lives to sanctify us in righteousness. By the help of that Spirit, we can choose to get rid of bitterness. Avoid rage. Extinguish anger. Stop brawling. Steer clear of slander. Reject malice. Beloved, God is still at work in you to make you holy, kind, compassionate, and forgiving. Welcome God's Spirit to transform your heart today.

God, my life is Yours. Show me where I am still choosing sin, and sanctify me by Your Spirit. I choose to cooperate with You so that I might be transformed more and more into the image of Christ. Amen.

Let Your Light Shine before Others

Be wise in the way you act toward outsiders; make the most of every opportunity. Let your conversation be always full of grace, seasoned with salt, so that you may know how to answer everyone.
COLOSSIANS 4:5–6

The most important rule of good writing is "*Show*, don't *tell*." When we're tracking along with a heroine's adventures in a story, we don't want the author to tell us that she was victorious. We want to experience what she did. We want to *see* it with our eyes. What we see is more compelling than what we're told. In his letter to the church at Colossae, Paul exhorts believers to be a people whose lives show Jesus to the world. He advises the body to be thoughtful about how they relate to those who aren't believers, encouraging them to make the most of every opportunity they have to influence others. Paul knows that the world won't be won over by sermons alone, but by the way they see believers living and speaking. Is your life a reflection of God's grace to those who don't know Him? Welcome God to work through you to bless others this week.

Lord, make my life a testimony to who You are. Through my speech and my actions, empower me to love those around me, in Jesus' name. Amen.

Loving God Means Loving Others

We love because he first loved us. Whoever claims to love God yet hates a brother or sister is a liar. For whoever does not love their brother and sister, whom they have seen, cannot love Goc whom they have not seen. And he has given us this commar Anyone who loves God must also love their brother and si

1 John 4:19–21

If you've ever heard a preacher spew hateful words ab particular person or group of people, you might be slow to believe th of what comes out of his or her mouth. Or if you've known a religio son who claims to be a Christian yet refuses to forgive a former sp r colleague, you might ask some legitimate questions about their f ecause we're human, we will have ruptures in our relationships wit ers. But the Christian life is still meant to be one marked by love fo and for others. John is saying that our love for others can never be rated from our love for God. The two are inextricably bound: if you God, you must love your brothers and sisters. Is there a relationsh your life that needs repair? Invite God to help you discern how best e another.

God, te to like You have loved me. Where my relationships are f or bruised, show me how to love well, in Jesus' name. Amen.

Jesus Knows What Our Lives Are Like

For surely it is not angels he helps, but Abraham's descendants. For this reason he had to be made like them, fully human in every way, in order that he might become a merciful and faithful high priest in service to God, and that he might make atonement for the sins of the people. Because he himself suffered when he was tempted, he is able to help those who are being tempted.

Hebrews 2:16–18

The complex mystery of Jesus' identity is that He is not just half and half, human and divine. In a way that we struggle to fathom, Jesus is both *fully* man and *fully* God. Oddly, the important part of that equation for our salvation is the human part! For Jesus to be a merciful and faithful priest—for Him to offer a perfect sacrifice—He needed to know what our lives are like. He had to know what it was, as a fully human man, to be tempted. And because He was tempted, just like we are, He can help us. We don't have a cosmic rescuer who doesn't know what it is to hunger for satisfaction, comfort, and pleasure. When you are tempted, notice Jesus' nearness. Invite His Spirit to fill you with power.

Lord, I thank You that You've experienced what I experience, but without sin. Because You know what my life is like, You are the merciful high priest I need today. Amen.

God Has Heard and Seen

"Go back and tell Hezekiah, the ruler of my people, 'This is what the Lord, the God of your father David, says: I have heard your prayer and seen your tears; I will heal you. On the third day from now you will go up to the temple of the Lord.' "

2 Kings 20:5

Jasmine was single for much longer than she would have chosen to be. She begged God to send her a husband, but God's plan was not unfolding according to her timeline. Karen, who'd been married for nine years, wrestled with infertility. For years she begged God to allow her to become a mother to a naturally born child. What have you been waiting for? Has it felt like God ignored your cries? Please know that He hears. Throughout scripture we see a God who notices the suffering of His children. Again an again we hear God assure sufferers, "I have heard. I have seen. I will intervene." What are you asking God for today? Continue to pray boldly with the confidence that God sees you. God hears you. God knows you. God loves you.

God, when I suffer, it feels as though You are far off. And I fear my prayers are hitting the ceiling and bouncing back down. Thank You for this reassurance that You are present to my pain today. I choose to trust that You are near and that You care. Amen.

A Prayer That Is for You

For this reason I kneel before the Father, from whom every family in heaven and on earth derives its name. I pray that out of his glorious riches he may strengthen you with power through his Spirit in your inner being, so that Christ may dwell in your hearts through faith. And I pray that you, being rooted and established in love, may have power, together with all the Lord's holy people, to grasp how wide and long and high and deep is the love of Christ, and to know this love that surpasses knowledge—that you may be filled to the measure of all the fullness of God.

Ephesians 3:14–19

When Paul was not able to be among the believers in Ephesus, he wrote them a letter expressing his heart and his concern for them. And in that letter Paul describes the prayer that he prayed for those followers of Christ. First, he prayed that they would be strengthened by the power of the Spirit so that Christ could flourish within them. Then he prayed that they would be able to understand the bigness—the width, length, height, and depth—of Christ's love for them. More than anything, Paul wanted the church to experience the big, big love of God and to be filled by Him. Today, echo the prayer that Paul prayed for the earliest believers.

Lord, by Your Spirit let Christ live and move in my heart today. And help me understand the expansive love of Christ for me. Amen.

You Need Not Live in Fear

And so we know and rely on the love God has for us. God is love. Whoever lives in love lives in God, and God in them. This is how love is made complete among us so that we will have confidence on the day of judgment: In this world we are like Jesus. There is no fear in love. But perfect love drives out fear, because fear has to do with punishment. The one who fears is not made perfect in love.

1 John 4:16–18

If you had a magic wand that could dissipate fear, wouldn't that be an amazing tool? You'd never have to be concerned about money. You wouldn't be afraid of your loved ones making bad choices for their lives. You'd never have to fear curious physical symptoms that would otherwise terrify you. (If you had this magic tool, you'd also probably be a zillionaire!) Well, John has actually discovered the secret to living without fear. He's learned that perfect love drives out fear. The two can't coexist. So, as you choose to live in love, to receive God's big, big love for you, you can trust in God's goodness. You might not have all the answers, and you still might not be able to control your circumstances, but you can have peace in the love God has for you. Today, you need not fear.

Father, I trust that You are God and I am not. I reject fear today, and I choose to rest in Your perfect love. Amen.

The Spirit Prays for You

For in this hope we were saved. But hope that is seen is no hope at all. Who hopes for what they already have? But if we hope for what we do not yet have, we wait for it patiently. In the same way, the Spirit helps us in our weakness. We do not know what we ought to pray for, but the Spirit himself intercedes for us through wordless groans. And he who searches our hearts knows the mind of the Spirit, because the Spirit intercedes for God's people in accordance with the will of God.

ROMANS 8:24–27

I'll bet you've had circumstances in your life when you didn't know how to pray. Maybe a friend was caught in an abusive marriage, and you had no idea how to pray for her. Or perhaps you were offered two different jobs and didn't know which one to ask God for. Or maybe you were seeking God's wisdom about the next step in your journey and felt overwhelmed by all of the variables involved. Beloved sister, the apostle Paul understands! In his letter to the Christ followers in Rome, he acknowledges that we *don't* know what to pray for. And the good news he offers is that we don't need to! The Spirit, Paul writes, helps us in our weakness by praying for us.

God, I thank You that I can come before You with all of my cares and concerns. Today I trust that You are listening as Your Holy Spirit prays on my behalf. Amen.

You Are Worthy to Serve God

Moses said to the Lord, "Pardon your servant, Lord. I have never been eloquent, neither in the past nor since you have spoken to your servant. I am slow of speech and tongue." The Lord said to him, "Who gave human beings their mouths? Who makes them deaf or mute? Who gives them sight or makes them blind? Is it not I, the Lord? Now go; I will help you speak and will teach you what to say."

Exodus 4:10–12

Just as God called Moses to speak on His behalf, God has called you to be a builder of His kingdom. If you have a sense of what it is that God has called you to do, you might—like Moses—have some reservations about the assignment! Maybe you lack the confidence or boldness to share the Gospel freely with others. Maybe you're worried about the financial repercussions of doing what you know God has told you to do. Or perhaps you fear missing out on something else if you say yes to God. Beloved, God's love and purpose for you are bigger than your fears. If God has called you to do it, the One who gives voice and sight will help you do what you were made to do.

Lord, You know the places in my life where I am afraid to follow You with boldness. You know how I am anxious about doing the thing for which I don't feel entirely equipped. But today I will step into Your calling for me and trust You to supply all I need, for Your glory. Amen.

You Are Enough

And that is what some of you were. But you were washed,
you were sanctified, you were justified in the name of
the Lord Jesus Christ and by the Spirit of our God.
1 Corinthians 6:11

The world bombards us with the message that we are not enough: we're not pretty enough, we're not fit enough, we're not smart enough, we're not clever enough. And on and on. We're even fed the lie that we're not *spiritual* enough! In his beautiful volume *The Inner Voice of Love*, Henri Nouwen gently exhorts, "But you know that is not God's voice." Beloved, the gentle voice of the Holy Spirit is faithful to help us discern between the voice that lies and the voice that tells the truth. As we listen to Paul's letter to the church in Corinth, we hear clearly the voice that does not lie. This is the voice that confirms the truth of your identity in Christ. It says, "You were washed. You were sanctified. You were justified." If you listen closely, you can hear God whispering in your ear, "You are *worthy*." You are! And the beautiful truth of your worthiness is that it does not depend on you. It depends entirely on Jesus. Jesus washed you. Jesus sanctified you. Jesus justified you. And because Jesus has redeemed you, you are *worthy*.

God, I thank You for Your true Word that confirms I am worthy. And thank You that the confidence I have doesn't depend on me but on Jesus. Help me stay rooted and grounded today in what is most true. Amen.

Remembering Who the Lord Has Been

The Lord *appeared to us in the past, saying: "I have loved you with an everlasting love; I have drawn you with unfailing kindness."*
Jeremiah 31:3

When there's a situation in our lives over which we have little control—a dream deferred, a wayward child, a health crisis, an injustice we are suffering, or even regular old loneliness—it is easy to become more concerned with ourselves than is healthy. We might be tempted to obsess on the situation that we don't have the power to change. In these moments or seasons when our vision is very myopic, God invites us to tilt our eyes toward Him and look at the bigger picture. When we remember who God has been in our lives and as we recall who God has been to His people over the generations, we can be set free from the bondage of being absorbed in ourselves. Jeremiah reminds a hurting people, "The Lord appeared to us in the past, saying, 'I have loved you with an everlasting love; I have drawn you with unfailing kindness.' " Beloved, as you open your eyes to God's steadfast faithfulness, notice who God has been in your life and in the lives of His people.

Lord, I confess that when I'm hurting, I focus on my own needs. Today I release them to You, and I remember all You have done in my life and in the lives of those who love You. Thank You that You have loved me with an everlasting love. Amen.

God Loved Us When We Were Still Sinners

But God demonstrates his own love for us in this:
While we were still sinners, Christ died for us.
Romans 5:8

Have you noticed how difficult it is to practice love toward those who are sinning? When a family member is caught up in addiction and all the brokenness and poor choices that accompany it, it can be hard to practice love toward them. When a friend has betrayed our confidence, it's difficult to feel love toward her. Or when a young adult child continually makes poor choices that cause harm to him and others, it can be difficult to love him. That's our natural human experience of love. But again and again, scripture teaches us that God's love is of a different order than human love. God doesn't love us only when we're being obedient. Or when we think we're getting things right. No, God chose to love when we were sinning. When we were behaving in ways that hurt us, hurt others, and hurt God, God *loved* us. That is the gracious nature of God's posture toward you and me today.

God, I thank You that Your love is unlike any human love I've experienced. I'm so grateful that You have found me worthy, because of Jesus, to receive Your steadfast, faithful love. Help me love those around me the way You have loved me. Amen.

God Will Give You What You Most Need

"The Most High will thunder from heaven; the LORD will judge the ends of the earth. He will give strength to his king and exalt the horn of his anointed."
1 SAMUEL 2:10

Many of us were raised in families where we were taught to work hard and achieve. If our families had few resources, we might have been taught to "pull ourselves up by our own bootstraps." Part of the story in our culture is that we can make of ourselves anything we choose. And this rugged individualism also suggests that we can do it on our own. But hustling hard to make a buck and achieving success by the sweat of our brow is a different narrative of human flourishing than we see in scripture. In the Bible, God promises to be with His people and to support us. A biblical anthropology acknowledges not only that we are weak and God is strong, but that God's strength is actually seen most powerfully *through our weakness.* Where do you need God's strength and support today? Ask God to strengthen and exalt you to do what you've been created to do.

Lord, I thank You that You are my rock and my strength. You know what is before me today, and I trust that You are equipping me to do what You've called me to do. I am Your servant. Amen.

I Will Be Their God, and They Will Be My People

"They will no longer defile themselves with their idols and vile images or with any of their offenses, for I will save them from all their sinful backsliding, and I will cleanse them. They will be my people, and I will be their God. . . . My dwelling place will be with them; I will be their God, and they will be my people."

Ezekiel 37:23, 27

Some of us have families who are spread out all over the country. If we grew up in the Midwest, our parents may have retired in Florida. If we are from the Southeast, a sibling may have gone to college in California or Washington State and set roots out west. Or maybe we started in the Southwest, and then after pursuing job opportunities in the Northeast, we may have planted ourselves there. We might long for the kind of geographic closeness and rootedness we see among families in other cultures, but we find ourselves isolated from those who know and love us the most. A lot of us find ourselves yearning for home, belonging, rootedness that goes beyond geography. And that's exactly what God promises us. God promises us both that we belong to Him and that He dwells with us. He lives inside the apartment, condo, or house where we lay our heads at night! God promises to be with us because we belong to Him.

God, I am hungry for a home that lasts. Thank You for promising to live with me. You are my God, and I am Your daughter. Amen.

This Is How God Showed His Love

This is how God showed his love among us: He sent his one and only Son into the world that we might live through him.
1 John 4:9

Have you ever had a day where you questioned God's love for you? Or maybe dozens of those days in a row? The enemy of our souls will often capitalize on the circumstances in our lives to make us question whether God really loves us. When a relationship fails, we wonder if God cares for us. When we face financial lack, we wonder if God notices our need. Or when things we'd hoped for fail to pass, we wonder if God loves us. And the answer we hear woven throughout the scriptures—to the chronic wondering whether we are loved by God—is a consistent yes! And in his little letter to the church, John offers definitive proof of God's love for them, for you, for me: "This is how God showed his love among us: He sent his one and only Son into the world that we might live through him." God has already done it! In sending Jesus, He communicated definitively His great love for us. So, when you're wondering, notice what Jesus has *already* done for you by coming into the world so that you could have life. God's love for you is sure, and it has already been accomplished and sealed.

Lord, I thank You for the great love You've poured out on me in the person of Jesus. Today I fix my mind on Your grace through Him. Amen.

God's Love Endures Forever

Give thanks to the Lord, *for he is good;*
his love endures forever.
1 Chronicles 16:34

One of the popular refrains we hear throughout scripture is the drumbeat of God's steadfast, faithful, enduring love. We hear it throughout the Old and New Testaments. In fact, the Hebrew word the Bible uses for "love," *hesed*, means so much more than the generic "love" that we use to describe our feelings for chocolate, movies, spouses, and daisies! *Hesed* implies a love that is steadfast, faithful, enduring. In Psalm 136—a song I wish I could hear in its original form!—the author ends every verse with the same refrain, "His love endures forever." And we hear the same refrain here in the book of 1 Chronicles. God's love endures forever. Can you imagine your life as a fabric tapestry, with the single thread woven throughout being that strain of God's steadfast, faithful love? When you pray, close your eyes and notice God's *hesed* woven throughout the seasons of your life. And give thanks to God today because His love *for you* endures forever.

God, Your unfailing love has been woven throughout my life. I give You thanks today because You love me. You have never behaved toward me in a manner that was anything other than good! So, I celebrate Your steadfast faithfulness to me and rest in Your love today. Amen.

God Passed By and Saw You

"Then I passed by and saw you kicking about in your blood, and as you lay there in your blood I said to you, 'Live!' "
EZEKIEL 16:6

If you haven't read it, the book of Ezekiel includes the most visceral, heartbreaking, beautiful story of an infant who is born to parents who do not care for her. Instead of cleaning or swaddling her, they simply leave her in an open field to die. They despise her. But the Lord walks by and speaks life to this infant. She grows and develops, and He covers her, making an oath of fidelity to her. He cleanses her and dresses her in the finest garments, adorning her with exquisite jewelry. He even feeds her the choicest foods. The story God speaks through Ezekiel is the story of His relationship with His people, and it is also a story of His relationship with you and me. God notices our need and enters our lives to care for us. Today God is saying to you, "Live!" Can you hear His voice? You are loved and worthy of the new life God offers you today.

God, I hear Your voice speaking life to me. Thank You for the tender care You offer me as You draw me into relationship with You. You are my good and faithful protector and my provider. Amen.

The Word of the Lord Endures Forever

For, "All people are like grass, and all their glory is like the flowers of the field; the grass withers and the flowers fall, but the word of the Lord endures forever." And this is the word that was preached to you.

1 Peter 1:24–25

When my grandfather died a few years ago at the age of ninety-seven, he'd lived a life that spanned the invention of the television when he was in middle school and eventually the mysterious magical wonders of the iPhone! The amount of technological change he witnessed in his lifetime was unprecedented in human history. And as we've all learned over the last decade or two, whatever is hot today—whether it's the way we play music, shop, or are entertained by screens—will most likely be outdated before we've got that new iPhone paid off. But a lot of us are reading a book about a very unlikely man that was written two thousand years ago. And parts of our Bible were recorded many hundreds of years before that! It's not just remarkable that we're reading and finding life in an old book, we're actually engaged with the Word of God that is active and alive. God's Word, as He has spoken it and as it's been recorded, endures forever. And you can find *life* in this living Word.

Lord, thank You for breathing life into the scriptures. By the power of the Holy Spirit, vivify me through Your Word that endures forever. Amen.

God's Banner over You Is Love

Let him lead me to the banquet hall,
and let his banner over me be love.
SONG OF SONGS 2:4

Scripture identifies the relationship between God and people several different ways. The two most prominent relational metaphors are familial ones: God is the parent who claims us as sons and daughters; God is the groom who takes the church as His holy bride. God is the Father who finds infant Jerusalem flailing in her own blood in Ezekiel 16, and God is the One who claims Jesus as His Son at Jesus' baptism. And just as He claimed Jesus as His beloved Child, God also claims us. The second image is that of a bride and groom, and the Song of Songs describes a love that is at times romantic and even erotic between a man and a woman. Whether you are single or married, know that God is the ultimate lover of your soul. It is as if He leads you into a great party and His banner over you is a declaration of His love. Beloved, you are completely loved—and completely *complete*—because you are loved by God with a love that does not fail.

Lord, You know that my insides yearn to be loved perfectly. I love to be loved as no human can love me. You promise to meet that deep need of my heart. Let me experience the richness and fullness of Your love today. Amen.

You Have Been Made for Freedom

To the Jews who had believed him, Jesus said, "If you hold to my teaching, you are really my disciples. Then you will know the truth, and the truth will set you free." They answered him, "We are Abraham's descendants and have never been slaves of anyone. How can you say that we shall be set free?" Jesus replied, "Very truly I tell you, everyone who sins is a slave to sin. Now a slave has no permanent place in the family, but a son belongs to it forever. So if the Son sets you free, you will be free indeed."

John 8:31–36

This conversation Jesus had with Jewish believers is kind of mind-bending. When He implies that they can be set free by truth, they protest that—because of their prestigious lineage—they've never been slaves to anyone. Somehow they don't yet understand that slavery means both metal-shackled forced labor and bondage to sin. Even after He spells it out, they protest that they are the children of Abraham. So. . .they really aren't getting it. Jesus longs for them to experience the fullness of spiritual freedom that comes from Him, and yet they see no need to be justified. Do you? Are you aware of your daily dependence on what Jesus has done for you? He has no business with those who are freely self-justified but gladly redeems those who know themselves to be bound and in need of a savior.

Jesus, my Redeemer, I thank You for setting me free from sin and death. Today I depend solely on what You have done for me. Through Your death and resurrection, I am free! Amen.

God Sees Your Pain

As he approached the town gate, a dead person was being carried out—the only son of his mother, and she was a widow. And a large crowd from the town was with her. When the Lord saw her, his heart went out to her and he said, "Don't cry."

LUKE 7:12–13

Gospel writer Luke describes a funeral procession marching past as Jesus approaches the city gate. It is a funeral of a young man who's been his mother's only son. And on top of that, the woman is widowed. So, it's fair to assume that this young man who died had been her whole world. And when Jesus sees her, his heart overflows with compassion. He notices her tears. And when you are sad, beloved, God sees your tears as well. With that confidence, offer God the hurts in your heart today.

Lord, I thank You that You not only see the hurts of our hearts, but You care. I do believe that when You notice the hurts I carry, Your heart overflows with compassion. Thank You for Your tender love for me. Amen.

He Satisfies the Thirsty and Fills the Hungry

Let them give thanks to the Lord for his unfailing love and his wonderful deeds for mankind, for he satisfies the thirsty and fills the hungry with good things.
Psalm 107:8–9

The Gospel of God has always meant different things for those who are wealthy, strong, and powerful and those who are poor, weak, and powerless. In the Gospels, we see wealthy Zacchaeus offer to hand over his wealth when he meets Jesus. And yet the folks who encountered Jesus that were poor were given hope that they would be fed and cared for by God's gracious hand. In case you haven't figured it out, God's justice—that at times requires sacrifice for the rich—is great news for the poor. God's promise to you and to me is that He satisfies the thirsty and fills the hungry with good things. Where do you find yourself hungry today? Where do you need God to meet your needs? Because God is your good provider, ask Him for what you need today.

Lord, I give You thanks for Your unfailing love. In seasons of plenty and in seasons of want, I know I can trust You to provide what I need. You are the gracious giver of all that is good. And just as You meet my needs, I ask You to continue to provide for those who are hungry, thirsty, and poor. In Jesus' name, amen.

God Brings Life Where There Is No Life

"I will attach tendons to you and make flesh come upon you and cover you with skin; I will put breath in you, and you will come to life. Then you will know that I am the Lord."
Ezekiel 37:6

When we see God showing Ezekiel a valley full of dry bones, we get to witness God doing what God does best: bringing life out of death. He instructs Ezekiel to speak to these dead bones, commanding them to live. It's a miracle we see God perform time after time in scripture. When Isaac was assigned to die, God rescued him. When Joseph's life was intended for death, God intervened. When Jesus raised a widow's son and Lazarus from the dead, we witness God bringing life from death. And in His ultimate sign of resurrection, God rescues Jesus from the jaws of hell. This is *what God does*. And it's how we know that God is God. Where have you seen God bring new life in your past? Where do you need God to bring life out of death today?

God, You have shown Yourself time and time again to be someone who raises the dead. Thank You for giving me new life in You. Continue to usher new life into my life. Amen.

God Sets You Free from Sinful Desires

So I say, walk by the Spirit, and you will not gratify the desires of the flesh. For the flesh desires what is contrary to the Spirit, and the Spirit what is contrary to the flesh. They are in conflict with each other, so that you are not to do whatever you want. But if you are led by the Spirit, you are not under the law.

GALATIANS 5:16–18

Though we each have our own unique struggles, we all have various temptations of the flesh. One friend of mine battles chronic overeating. She knows how to make healthy choices, but—as if against her will—she chooses deliciousness that she knows is harming her body. Another friend wrestles with drinking too much alcohol. She has seasons where she can avoid alcohol altogether, but then her mind plays tricks on her and she suddenly slips into overuse. And many of us choose to gratify desires of the flesh that we think we can hide from others: Netflix binging, pornography, shopping, and more. We know firsthand that the flesh desires what is contrary to the Spirit. But Paul assures the church in Galatia that we have what it takes to walk in the Spirit and not gratify the desires of the flesh. Ask God to set you free from the law's power today by empowering you by His Spirit.

God, You know my unique temptations to give in to the desires of the flesh. But I also believe that You have equipped me to walk in Your power by the Spirit. Be my helper today. Amen.

Seek God's Wisdom

Better to be lowly in spirit along with the oppressed than to share plunder with the proud. Whoever gives heed to instruction prospers, and blessed is the one who trusts in the Lord. The wise in heart are called discerning, and gracious words promote instruction.

Proverbs 16:19–21

Throughout the scriptures, and especially in the book of Proverbs, the virtues of wisdom are extolled. Proverbs helps us glean how pursuing wisdom helps us to live *well*. The woman who lives wisely prospers because she heeds instruction. When her friends give her feedback, when her boss corrects her, when her teacher schools her, she is quick to listen, learn, and correct. The wise woman who learns from others is called *discerning*. Do you have this openhearted posture that seeks to learn and grow when others give you feedback? Are you quick to listen and slow to put up defensive walls? God's heart for you is that you would grow in wisdom, and God often uses the people around us to help us get there. When you pray, ask God to grant you wisdom.

Lord, You know I want to become the woman You made me to be. Teach me what it means to walk in the way of wisdom, and soften my spirit to receive instruction from others. Amen.

God's Kindness Leads You to Repentance

So when you, a mere human being, pass judgment on them and yet do the same things, do you think you will escape God's judgment? Or do you show contempt for the riches of his kindness, forbearance and patience, not realizing that God's kindness is intended to lead you to repentance?
ROMANS 2:3–4

In his letter to the believers in Rome, Paul calls out those in the body who are judging others. And he has the insight to notice that the things they're judging are the very things they're doing themselves! Notice this natural human tendency the next time you judge someone for their driving, their speaking, their spending, or their. . .anything. It's how we are, right? And yet Paul names this graceless judgment we practice as showing contempt for the riches of God's kindness, forbearance, and patience. It's as if he's begging them, "Don't you get it? God's kindness toward *you* is meant to cause you to be transformed. So when you judge others, it's kind of like you're spitting in God's face!" When you pray, ask God's Spirit to show you when you're cheapening God's big grace for you by judging others. And let that humility lead you to repentance.

God, I am overwhelmed by Your kindness to me. Forgive me when I squander it by judging others. Lord, transform me by Your Spirit so that I might practice the generous kindness You've offered me. Amen.

What God Values Often Surprises Us

His pleasure is not in the strength of the horse, nor his delight in the legs of the warrior; the Lord delights in those who fear him, who put their hope in his unfailing love.

Psalm 147:10–11

People in the ancient world valued different things than we value today. They didn't have lightning-quick sports cars, but they did value the strength of a horse. They didn't have CrossFit gym memberships, but they did value the legs of a warrior. But the psalmist reminds us that what people value is not what God values. It's not what causes Him to delight in us. What causes God to delight in us is counterintuitive when measured against the world's values. "The Lord," the psalmist assures us, "delights in those who fear him, who put their hope in his unfailing love." What will it look like today for you to hope in God's unfailing love? (Hint: it most likely means you won't have to bank on that sports car or CrossFit to realize your value!)

Lord, I confess that I am tempted to trust in what offers me earthly security and comfort and prestige. But I read in scripture that You have turned the world's values on their head! So, today I put my hope in Your unfailing love for me. I trust in nothing less. Amen.

So the Works of God Might Be Displayed

"Neither this man nor his parents sinned," said Jesus, "but this happened so that the works of God might be displayed in him. As long as it is day, we must do the works of him who sent me. Night is coming, when no one can work. While I am in the world, I am the light of the world."

John 9:3–5

Sometimes scripture offends my modern sensibilities, and this conversation between Jesus and a crowd gathered around a man born blind is one of those passages. It begins when Jesus' disciples, who'd been taught to believe that people suffer because they have sinned, want to know if this guy was blind because he had sinned or because his parents had sinned. To their ears, it was a legitimate question. But Jesus told them that neither was true! This happened, Jesus explained, "So that the works of God might be displayed in him." To my ear, that's almost as rough as the other two options! But again and again, both in the lives of people Jesus touches in scripture and also in lives of folks who've met Him today, we see Jesus redeeming brokenness for God's glory. Perhaps there's even a situation in your life today that you wouldn't have chosen but that Jesus is using to glorify God.

Father of Jesus, Your ways confound me! Although I don't understand all the reasons people suffer, I do trust Your Word and I have seen You redeem the most difficult circumstances. Amen.

Expect to See God's Goodness

I remain confident of this: I will see the goodness of the LORD in the land of the living. Wait for the LORD; be strong and take heart and wait for the LORD.
PSALM 27:13–14

Those of us who've put our trust in Jesus have an eternal hope that when we die, we'll spend eternity with God in heaven. And even though we can't quite wrap our minds around what that entails, we have the confidence that it's gonna be *good*. Amen? Even when death takes the lives of those we love, we have the promise that, ultimately, death does not win. But the psalmist who penned Psalm 27 has a hope in God that lives closer to home. This child of God believes that he or she will see God's goodness in the land of the living. *Before* death. And this hope infuses my faith with hope that I will taste God's goodness *in this life*. So, the psalmist exhorts us to wait patiently for the Lord, and that kind of waiting takes courage. This is a beautiful prayer to pray to God when you are desperate to taste His goodness in this life: "Lord, I wait for You. I am strengthened and take heart as I wait for You."

God, You know the deep needs and desires of my heart. So I put all of my trust in You. Come quickly because I wait for You. Amen.

When You Ask, God Hears

I write these things to you who believe in the name of the Son of God so that you may know that you have eternal life. This is the confidence we have in approaching God: that if we ask anything according to his will, he hears us. And if we know that he hears us—whatever we ask—we know that we have what we asked of him.

1 John 5:13–15

Have you ever prayed for something and wondered if your prayers were reaching God's ears? Have you prayed silent or spoken prayers toward God in heaven and feared that they were hitting the ceiling and just bouncing back? This little letter from John assures us that if we ask anything according to God's will, *He hears us*. Sister, this is big. This is really big. If we truly believe we've been heard, and we truly believe that God is who God says He is—gracious, loving, merciful, and kind—then we can be confident that a God who loves us will answer our prayers. When I'm honest, it scares me a little bit to pray that boldly! But we are invited to trust God with reckless abandon, believing that He hears and answers our prayers.

Lord, You have shown Yourself to be a gracious God. Thank You that when I pray, Your ears are open! Hear the prayers of my heart and the prayers of my lips, and I will await Your good provision. Amen.

God's Blessing Is upon You

"The LORD bless you and keep you; the LORD make his face shine on you and be gracious to you; the LORD turn his face toward you and give you peace."
NUMBERS 6:24–26

When God gave the law to His people, He spoke to Moses a prayer of blessing and instructed Moses to command Aaron and his sons to use the prayer to bless the Israelites. It was a liturgical prayer that they would use over and over. It was also a prayer that a number of songwriters set to music, including Michael Card, who has beautifully set the song to music in an album of holy lullabies! The prayer God gives has three parts. First, "The LORD bless you and keep you." Second, "The LORD make his face shine on you and be gracious to you." Finally, "The LORD turn his face toward you and give you peace." You'll notice that the blessing God gives is not riches, power, or fame. No, the blessing God bestows on the people He loves is His own presence. As you receive this blessing today, notice God's face shining upon you and giving you peace.

Lord, You are gracious. Bless me and keep me. Make Your face to shine upon me and be gracious to me. Turn Your face toward me and give me peace. Amen.

When We Follow Jesus, We Serve

Jesus knew that the Father had put all things under his power, and that he had come from God and was returning to God; so he got up from the meal, took off his outer clothing, and wrapped a towel around his waist. After that, he poured water into a basin and began to wash his disciples' feet, drying them with the towel that was wrapped around him.

John 13:3–5

On the night He was betrayed, Jesus ate supper with His friends and then surprised them by standing from the table, taking off His robe, wrapping a towel around His waist, and washing their feet. And what we might not grasp across generations and cultures is that this was the task of a lowly servant—not the work of a revered teacher and leader. In fact, Simon Peter's first instinct was to refuse to let Jesus wash his feet. But Jesus stooped before Peter and all the other disciples and washed their feet. Afterward, He explained to them what He'd done, encouraging them to imitate His act of service. The snapshot from that evening, of course, is like a thumbnail sketch of Jesus' entire ministry—taking the nature of servant for the sake of others. Jesus invites you and I to imitate Him by living as servants as well.

God, I confess that most often I'd prefer to be served than to serve. But I hear Your voice calling me to serve others just as You have. Give me opportunities to humble myself and serve in Your name today. Amen.

God Sent the One Who Saves

For to us a child is born, to us a son is given, and the government will be on his shoulders. And he will be called Wonderful Counselor, Mighty God, Everlasting Father, Prince of Peace. Of the greatness of his government and peace there will be no end. He will reign on David's throne and over his kingdom, establishing and upholding it with justice and righteousness from that time on and forever. The zeal of the LORD Almighty will accomplish this.

ISAIAH 9:6–7

In the Old Testament, the Jews trusted God for their redemption. But what they expected was someone more like a mighty king who would wage war and rule over neighboring nations than one who washed His friends' feet. When Isaiah predicts the coming of God's Anointed One, his prophecy would have challenged the idea of the powerful ruler the Israelites expected to save them. Yet, with hindsight, we are able to recognize today that God's announcement through Isaiah was anticipating the birth and reign of Jesus, who came as a child and was identified as God's own Son. Who reigns not only on David's throne—a symbol of God's own rule—but also in heaven with God. Though God's ancient people couldn't see clearly enough to recognize who was to come, we have seen this Promised One clearly in the person of Jesus.

Lord, You are a God of unlikely surprises. Thank You for coming into the world in ways that confound us, and thank You for making good on Your promise to send us a Savior. Amen.

God Does Not Desert You

"They refused to listen and failed to remember the miracles you performed among them. They became stiff-necked and in their rebellion appointed a leader in order to return to their slavery. But you are a forgiving God, gracious and compassionate, slow to anger and abounding in love. Therefore you did not desert them."

NEHEMIAH 9:17

A lot of us are willing to believe that when we met Jesus, our sins were forgiven, and we might even walk in mostly righteous ways in the glorious wake of our salvation. But as days and years tick by, we find ourselves tangled up once again in sin. We forget God's goodness toward us, and we become rebellious. Against all reason—and yet very much in keeping with our fallen human nature!—we return to the bondage of sin. The enemy hijacks our minds in an attempt to convince us that we're no longer forgiven. We're no longer saved. We're no longer God's. So Nehemiah, speaking to God, announces what is most true: "You are a forgiving God, gracious and compassionate, slow to anger and abounding in love." When you notice that you are feeling as though God's grace is far from you, repeat those true words and celebrate God's steadfast, faithful character toward you.

Lord, I confess that I have sinned. But I refuse the devil's logic that You do not forgive me. You are forgiving, gracious, and compassionate. You are slow to anger and abounding in love. Thank You for who You are. Amen.

Finding Peace in Plenty and in Want

I know what it is to be in need, and I know what it is to have plenty.
I have learned the secret of being content in any and every situation,
whether well fed or hungry, whether living in plenty or in want.
I can do all this through him who gives me strength.
PHILIPPIANS 4:12–13

Do you ever feel sort of bullied by your circumstances? Do you feel like some of the stuff going on in your life volleys you about like a beach ball bouncing on ocean waves? Because we all face challenges, we can learn how to ride those waves from Paul in this letter to believers in Philippi. Paul enjoyed all the perks of being a leader in the Jewish community before he encountered Jesus and sacrificed his reputation and livelihood to love and follow Him. Paul writes that he knows what it is to have plenty and he also knows what it is to be in need. He points to the secret of being content in any situation: depending not on his own strength or resources, which can come and go, but on the strength of God. Paul is convinced that no matter what his circumstances, he can survive and thrive with the help of God, in Christ.

God, You know what my circumstances have been, what they are, and what they will be. In all things, I put my trust in You, believing that You give me power to do everything You ask of me. Strengthen me today. Amen.

God Has Not Forgotten His Covenant with You

"Yet I will remember the covenant I made with you in the days of your youth, and I will establish an everlasting covenant with you."
Ezekiel 16:60

Do you remember the beginning of your life with God? Maybe you were baptized as a baby. Or maybe you made a commitment to Jesus as a child or teenager. Or perhaps your life was swept up by God's Spirit as an adult. However it happened, God made a covenant with you to be your God. In this unbreakable promise, God vowed to be your faithful rock and protector. God first made this covenant promise to His chosen people. But when they were in exile, they began to wonder whether God had broken the covenant He'd made. So, in this prophecy from Ezekiel, when God's people were hurting and wondering whether God cared for them, God assured His people that He remembered the covenant He made. He hadn't forgotten that He promised to be their God. Even when their circumstances looked dicey, God promised Israel that He remembered His everlasting covenant.

Lord, You have shown Yourself to Your people and to me as a God of steadfast covenant faithfulness. I trust You to honor Your covenant to be my God. I rejoice that I belong to You and that my life is in Your hands. Teach me to trust You today and to follow more closely in Your footsteps. Amen.

Do Everything in a Way That Glorifies God

Do everything without grumbling or arguing, so that you may become blameless and pure, "children of God without fault in a warped and crooked generation." Then you will shine among them like stars in the sky as you hold firmly to the word of life. And then I will be able to boast on the day of Christ that I did not run or labor in vain.

PHILIPPIANS 2:14–16

Have you ever watched a child respond to a parent who expected him or her to be obedient? Sometimes a child can obey her parent with earnestness and sincerity. And other times a child might balk, resisting his parents' words. He might do what they asked, but with an ugly spirit and attitude. In his letter to believers in Philippi, Paul exhorts the body to "do everything without grumbling or arguing." Like many parents, Paul understood that the spirit in which the body behaved was as important as the obedience itself! And he promised that when they did, they would shine like stars in the universe. As their father, coach, and teacher, he poured into them work that would be validated, and he would be able to boast about them. As you respond to God, are you able to do it with a willing spirit?

God, You know I long to be faithful to You. As I respond in obedience to You, give me a joyful spirit. It is my privilege to know, love, and serve You. May I live so faithfully to You that I can boast on the day of Christ! Amen.

God Is with You in Your Most Difficult Days

"But you, Israel, my servant, Jacob, whom I have chosen, you descendants of Abraham my friend, I took you from the ends of the earth, from its farthest corners I called you. I said, 'You are my servant'; I have chosen you and have not rejected you. So do not fear, for I am with you; do not be dismayed, for I am your God. I will strengthen you and help you; I will uphold you with my righteous right hand."

ISAIAH 41:8–10

On the day that we coordinate the church picnic and see everyone enjoy fellowshipping together, it's easy to believe that God is with us. Or when we finally gather our courage to share the Gospel with a colleague at work, and that friend accepts Christ, we see God's presence and provision on the journey. But when we feel as though we've been abandoned by God, when we feel like we're in exile, it is harder to recognize God's steadfast presence with us. Yet it was in Israel's darkest day, and in ours, that God speaks, "Do not fear, for I am with you; do not be dismayed, for I am your God." When we need Him most, God promises to help us. If you doubt God's presence in your dark days, close your eyes and ask Him to show His face. He is *with you*.

Lord, thank You that You have called me worthy of Your love. Worthy of Your help. Worthy of Your presence. Open my eyes to see You present with me in my most difficult days. Amen.

God Is Your Daddy Who Loves You

Therefore, brothers and sisters, we have an obligation—but it is not to the flesh, to live according to it. For if you live according to the flesh, you will die; but if by the Spirit you put to death the misdeeds of the body, you will live. For those who are led by the Spirit of God are the children of God. The Spirit you received does not make you slaves, so that you live in fear again; rather, the Spirit you received brought about your adoption to sonship. And by him we cry, "Abba, Father."

ROMANS 8:12–15

When you talk to God, what kind of language do you use? Is it formal and proper, like "Lord" or "Father"? Or is it more intimate, like "Daddy" or "Abba"? Though used just three times in the New Testament, once by Jesus and twice by Paul, the word *Abba* is the Aramaic word for "father." In each usage, the speaker is implying a particularly intimate relationship with God the Father. If you long for that kind of intimacy with the One who loves you, consider praying using the word *Abba* to underscore God's tender, fatherly love for you.

Abba, I thank You that You are the Father who does not fail. So, I come to You with complete assurance that You are my loving Daddy. Today I put my trust in You. Amen.

The Prudent See Danger and Take Refuge

Rich and poor have this in common: The LORD is the Maker of them all. The prudent see danger and take refuge, but the simple keep going and pay the penalty. Humility is the fear of the LORD; its wages are riches and honor and life.

PROVERBS 22:2–4

Our natural temptation when we see something alluring is to be drawn to it. If we're dieting, it might be a soft, gooey, freshly baked chocolate chip cookie. If we're dating, it might be a very attractive man whose character leaves much to be desired. If we're watching our spending, chances are good that we'll see an ad on social media for something absolutely irresistible. And each of these poses a danger to staying the course we've set for ourselves. Proverbs says that the prudent *see danger* and *take refuge*, while the simple keep going and pay the penalty. What's your response when you're tempted? Is your first reaction "Well, a little bit won't hurt," or is it "I'm going to step back even further from this one"? You practice walking in the way of wisdom when you take refuge from whatever endangers your obedience to God.

Lord, I long to be faithful to You. Open my eyes to danger, and give me the courage to flee from temptation. May You be glorified in all I do. Amen.

Difficulties Grow Us into People of Hope

Not only so, but we also glory in our sufferings, because we know that suffering produces perseverance; perseverance, character; and character, hope. And hope does not put us to shame, because God's love has been poured out into our hearts through the Holy Spirit, who has been given to us.

Romans 5:3–5

When friends of mine have been in the midst of cancer treatments, it's been hard to find the bright side of the grueling process. Similarly, those enduring the end of a marriage find it hard to name the good side of that season. When we're suffering, it's hard to see much further than our noses. But Paul suggests that, for the believer, something more is going on. In a rhythmic crescendo, he claims that suffering produces perseverance in us. And perseverance produces character. And then he has the audacity to suggest that character produces *hope*. It's been true in my experience that although I had little hope while suffering, God did redeem it in the ways Paul names. "And hope does not put us to shame," Paul insists, "because God's love has been poured out into our hearts through the Holy Spirit."

God, I thank You that my suffering has not been meaningless. You have been at work in my life, making me stronger and growing me more and more into the image of Christ. Thank You for Your Holy Spirit on whom I can depend. Amen.

The World's Values Are Turned Upside Down

Who, being in very nature God, did not consider equality with God something to be used to his own advantage; rather, he made himself nothing by taking the very nature of a servant, being made in human likeness. And being found in appearance as a man, he humbled himself by becoming obedient to death—even death on a cross!

PHILIPPIANS 2:6–8

The woman with the most beautiful body wins. The man with the most money in the bank wins. The one with the most academic degrees wins. The fanciest cars. The biggest house. The most extravagant vacations. You and I know what it is that our culture esteems. In fact, we're bombarded daily by the world's values. But just as Jesus turned death on its head in His resurrection, He also inverted the world's measure of success and happiness. Jesus modeled the life-giving way for us by choosing to release His God-ness in order to take on our humanity. Jesus chose to be like us and chose to serve others to show us the good way. As you pattern your life after Jesus, how are you imitating the way of self-giving that He modeled?

Lord Jesus, I believe that I am being transformed to be more like You. Empower me today to choose the way You walked. Teach me to become a servant who lives like You. Amen.

God Cares for Those Who Trust Him

The LORD is good, a refuge in times of trouble.
He cares for those who trust in him.
NAHUM 1:7

The book of Nahum announces the impending downfall of the mighty Assyrian empire, one of Israel's most feared oppressors. Reminding God's people of how God behaved in the past, Nahum signals that a God who loves justice will thwart the evil empire. And the story Nahum tells about the fall of Assyria's capital, Nineveh, is sort of like a continuation of God's judgment on the city in the time of Jonah. When people couldn't yet see how such a mighty bully of an enemy could be defeated, God spoke a word of promise and hope. God's people know what it is to have been dwarfed and dominated by the great nation, and they're longing for freedom and release. Nahum assures God's people, "The LORD is good, a refuge in times of trouble. He cares for those who trust in him." If any had lost heart, Nahum—whose name means "comfort"—reassures them that God cares for them. When you face trouble, do you seek refuge in God?

Lord, thank You for being a God of justice. And thank You that in the midst of trouble I can find refuge in Your care. Today I place my trust in You. Amen.

This Is My Command: Love Each Other

"You are my friends if you do what I command. I no longer call you servants, because a servant does not know his master's business. Instead, I have called you friends, for everything that I learned from my Father I have made known to you. You did not choose me, but I chose you and appointed you so that you might go and bear fruit—fruit that will last—and so that whatever you ask in my name the Father will give you. This is my command: Love each other."

John 15:14–17

At the end of Jesus' ministry, He spoke openly with the disciples about who He was and why He'd come. In His absence, that they didn't yet understand, He wanted them to know how to live faithfully as His followers. He assured them that they were more than servants; they were friends, since He passed on to them everything He received from the Father. Jesus commissions them to continue in ministry, bearing lasting fruit. And the pressing command, the one He reiterates throughout the end of John's Gospel, is simple: love each other. It's like the big takeaway that Jesus is impressing on the hearts of His friends: *I want you to love each other.*

Jesus, I hear the words that You spoke to Your friends.
Teach me how to love the friends You've given me so
that we might bear kingdom fruit that lasts. Amen.

The Lord Has Your Back

The LORD watches over you—the LORD is your shade at your right hand; the sun will not harm you by day, nor the moon by night. The LORD will keep you from all harm—he will watch over your life; the LORD will watch over your coming and going both now and forevermore.

PSALM 121:5–8

One friend I know lies awake at night worrying about tasks from her job that she left undone the previous day. Another is up in the middle of the night concerned about a child who's making really poor choices with his life. And another is alert in bed at night plagued by generalized anxiety. Each finds it hard to shut off the worries in her mind. But the psalmist promises that the Lord is standing on duty. When we're horizontal—and when we're vertical!—God watches over our lives. This doesn't mean that harm won't befall us. But it does mean when the dreaded phone call or knock on the door comes in the middle of the night, the Lord is with us, now and forevermore. Beloved, God is One to whom you can release every care in your heart.

God, I trust that the sun will not harm me by day nor the moon by night because You are my vigilant protector. Today I release my cares to You because You can be trusted. I rest in Your care now and forevermore. Amen.

God Builds a New Family

He replied to him, "Who is my mother, and who are my brothers?" Pointing to his disciples, he said, "Here are my mother and my brothers. For whoever does the will of my Father in heaven is my brother and sister and mother."

MATTHEW 12:48–50

When Jesus was speaking to a crowd, someone alerted Him that His mother and brothers were waiting outside to see Him. And His answer wasn't one that would have been popular with either His family or His culture! He asked, "Who is my mother, and who are my brothers?" And Jesus continued to teach that whoever did the will of His Father in heaven was His family member. In the larger canon of the New Testament, we hear the imperative to prioritize care of family members. But Jesus was doing something different here: He was naming a new kind of family. He was naming a bond between His followers, knit together by love for His Father, that was as strong as any blood tie. Look for these precious relationships in the beloved sisters and brothers God has given you.

God, I thank You for the brothers and sisters in Christ You have given me. In our devotion to You, our bond is strong. Teach me what it means that You are my primary allegiance, and teach me to love well. Amen.

God Knows All of Your Days

My frame was not hidden from you when I was made in the secret place, when I was woven together in the depths of the earth. Your eyes saw my unformed body; all the days ordained for me were written in your book before one of them came to be.
Psalm 139:15–16

Some people who aren't really baby people start relating more to little ones when they are finally able to walk and talk. For them, that's when an infant becomes a "real person." Others bond with babies the moment they leave the womb, citing the time and date of their birth as their official beginning. And still others mark life beginning at the moment of conception. Similarly, the psalmist hearkens back to that season when God knit him together in the womb. The writer cites not only God's handiwork and oversight, but also God's knowledge and ordination of every subsequent day of life that would be lived. When you consider the last few days of your life, is it easy or difficult to imagine that God knew each one before they unfolded? I find peace and confidence in that promise—that nothing in my life surprises God!

Lord, You knew every one of my days before even one of them came to be. I trust that I have been held in Your love during every one. Thank You that You know me intimately and that You care for me. Amen.

The One Who Knows Everything You've Ever Done

Many of the Samaritans from that town believed in him because of the woman's testimony, "He told me everything I ever did." So when the Samaritans came to him, they urged him to stay with them, and he stayed two days. And because of his words many more became believers. They said to the woman, "We no longer believe just because of what you said; now we have heard for ourselves, and we know that this man really is the Savior of the world."

John 4:39–42

Only one Gospel writer, John, relays the story of Jesus' encounter with a Samaritan woman at a well. The fact is Jesus should never have been talking with her. What John's first readers would have known is that Samaritans were despised by Jews. And in their odd encounter, Jesus reveals something to her about her life that she hadn't told Him—that she'd had five husbands, and the one she had currently wasn't her husband. Now, whenever someone calls me out on *my* sin, I put walls up pretty fast. But the way I know that Jesus spoke to her with a gracious and loving countenance is because she was awestruck by His knowledge and ran and told her neighbors about Him! When I close my eyes, I think I can see the face and hear the voice that would have made her feel seen, received, and accepted rather than dismissed and rejected. And it is *beautiful*.

God, the way You received a Samaritan woman and the way You receive me is amazing. Today, let me see Your face and hear Your voice. Amen.

I Am with You and Will Rescue You

"Alas, Sovereign LORD," I said, "I do not know how to speak; I am too young." But the LORD said to me, "Do not say, 'I am too young.' You must go to everyone I send you to and say whatever I command you. Do not be afraid of them, for I am with you and will rescue you," declares the LORD.

JEREMIAH 1:6–8

Throughout scripture, we are introduced to people who've been called by God but who are reticent to step forth into their calling. When God called Moses, who had a speech impediment, he tried to dodge God's plan. Here, Jeremiah has received God's call and yet protests that he is too young. But both men learned what I suspect you have as well: God's plans are not thwarted by our protests! God insists that Jeremiah go wherever he is sent and speak whatever God commands. As He did with Moses and as He does for us, God assured Jeremiah that he need not fear because God would be with him. Have you heard that voice in your life, assuring you, "Do not be afraid of them, for I am with you and will rescue you"? In life's greatest challenges, God promises to be with us and for us.

Lord, thank You for Your presence with me today.
As I step into whatever You have for me, I believe
that You are with me and You are for me. Amen.

Because of God's Mercy

But when the kindness and love of God our Savior appeared, he saved us, not because of righteous things we had done, but because of his mercy. He saved us through the washing of rebirth and renewal by the Holy Spirit.
TITUS 3:4–5

When life is hard, we wonder if God is good. When the relationship we so yearned for ends, we wonder. When we struggle with a family member, we wonder. When our lives do not unfold as we imagined they would, we wonder. Beloved, the God we discover in scripture, the One we meet in the Old Testament and come to know more deeply in Christ, is revealed as a God who is *good*. He saved us not because we did anything particularly deserving but because He is merciful. In the little letter that Paul wrote to Titus, he confirms that God is kind and loving. But the naughty voice of the enemy casts a shadow of doubt in our hearts and minds about God's goodness. When you hear that hiss, return to this scripture and speak it aloud. Agree with Paul that we worship a God who is kind, loving, and merciful.

God, I confess that I'm tempted to doubt Your goodness when life is hard. So, I cling to Your Word and agree that You are good. You are loving. You are kind. You are merciful. Amen.

You Are Worthy of God's Banquet Feast

"Then he said to his servants, 'The wedding banquet is ready, but those I invited did not deserve to come. So go to the street corners and invite to the banquet anyone you find.' So the servants went out into the streets and gathered all the people they could find, the bad as well as the good, and the wedding hall was filled with guests."

MATTHEW 22:8–10

Most women I know who use social media, both younger ones and older ones, have gotten to a point where they've needed to take a break from the constant stream of other people's elegant dinner parties, and beautiful children, and sterling spouses, and airbrush-quality selfies. Even when our lives are rich with loving relationships, getting a peek at the most polished glimpses of others' lives can make us feel like we're missing out. When Jesus describes the kind of banquet God throws, He makes it clear that it's not just the well-heeled elite who will be there. God is searching high and low to make sure that the hall is filled. And God longs for you to eat at His table, receiving His goodness and celebrating His glory. Say yes to spending time in His presence today.

God, You know I long to be fully included and received. Your Word bears witness that You are not only a God who welcomes all to the table, but You are the Good Shepherd who goes out and seeks the lost. Thank You for Your invitation. I will enjoy Your presence today. Amen.

Give Thanks to Him and Praise His Name

Enter his gates with thanksgiving and his courts with praise;
give thanks to him and praise his name. For the Lord is good and his love
endures forever; his faithfulness continues through all generations.
Psalm 100:4–5

In the last decade or two, a lot of people have been touting the benefits of gratitude. Oprah Winfrey has been a chief advocate of the power and pleasure of practicing gratitude. For ten years, she kept a journal of gratitude, naming all the things for which she was grateful. When she kept that journal, she noticed and experienced the joy of simple moments. In Psalm 100, the psalmist not only exhorts the reader to express gratitude, but the writer also points to the One worthy of our thanks and praise. As God's people, we are invited to thank God for His gifts and praise His name. Whether you pen it in a journal or shout it from the rooftops, what are you thanking God for today? As you pray, list specific gifts, opportunities, people, and possibilities for which you are thanking God.

Lord, You are the One who is worthy of all my praise and thanksgiving. Today I worship You because You are good and Your love endures forever. Your faithfulness continues through all generations. Thank You for the small and large blessings in my life that I receive as good gifts from You. Amen.

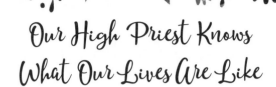

Our High Priest Knows What Our Lives Are Like

Therefore, since we have a great high priest who has ascended into heaven, Jesus the Son of God, let us hold firmly to the faith we profess. For we do not have a high priest who is unable to empathize with our weaknesses, but we have one who has been tempted in every way, just as we are—yet he did not sin. Let us then approach God's throne of grace with confidence, so that we may receive mercy and find grace to help us in our time of need.

HEBREWS 4:14–16

During the first few centuries of the church, believers wrestled to understand and name the ways in which Christ was divine and the ways in which He was human. One person being God and man was a knotty concept that caused disagreements in the early church. At a church council in Chalcedon though, leaders agreed together that Christ was fully God and fully human. And although the church has upheld the teaching for the many centuries since then, it's still a lot for us to wrap our minds around today! But it matters deeply for your life and mine. It means that we have a mediator who knows what our lives are like. Jesus knows what it is to be hungry, to be tempted, and to trust in what His Father provides. So, we can approach God with confidence!

God, thank You that You chose to take on flesh to be with us. And thank You that You know what my life is like. You are a mighty and merciful high priest. Amen.

You Need Not Be Afraid

The Lord is my light and my salvation—whom shall I fear?
The Lord is the stronghold of my life—of whom shall I be afraid? . . .
One thing I ask from the Lord, this only do I seek: that I may
dwell in the house of the Lord all the days of my life, to gaze
on the beauty of the Lord and to seek him in his temple.
Psalm 27:1, 4

The author of Psalm 27 is facing fierce enemies. But during enemy attack from his foes, he asks just one thing from God: *to be with Him*. The psalmist yearns to dwell in God's house and to be in His presence. Isn't that a beautiful contrast? I can almost see enemies banging on the door of God's house, and the psalmist is peacefully nestled up beside his Maker who keeps him safe. The psalmist knows where to go for safety, comfort, and peace. Do you? Sometimes it feels easier to reach for a pint of ice cream or glass of wine than it does to pause and get grounded in God's presence. But that is where peace is found. So whatever attacks might be barraging you today, know that there is a safe home where God is waiting for you.

Lord, You are my light and my salvation. There is nothing I fear. You are the stronghold of my life. Today I choose to remain rooted and grounded in Your steadfast holy presence. Amen.

A Father Who Gives Good Gifts

"Which of you, if your son asks for bread, will give him a stone? Or if he asks for a fish, will give him a snake? If you, then, though you are evil, know how to give good gifts to your children, how much more will your Father in heaven give good gifts to those who ask him!"
MATTHEW 7:9–11

Some of us received bad gifts when we were children. I don't mean knockoff Legos or dollar-store Barbies. I mean that God made us to be *loved well*, and some of us had parents who weren't equipped to do that. Maybe a parent left our childhood home. Or maybe one died. Perhaps a parent drank too much. Or battled mental illness. Or had a raging temper. No human parent can love us perfectly, the way we were intended to be loved. So it's natural that we might quietly suspect that God's love is like the parent who left or the one who stayed. But Jesus wants us to know in our deep places that God's love is of an entirely different order than human love. Though human love fails, God's love does not fail. In fact, God delights in giving good gifts to those who ask Him. If your heart is hungry for the love of a good Father, you have one now.

Abba, today I am bold to ask You for good gifts. Thank You for loving me with a perfect love. Help me to release the hurts of the past and to trust You for a good future. Amen.

Nothing Can Separate Us from God's Love

No, in all these things we are more than conquerors through him who loved us. For I am convinced that neither death nor life, neither angels nor demons, neither the present nor the future, nor any powers, neither height nor depth, nor anything else in all creation, will be able to separate us from the love of God that is in Christ Jesus our Lord.

Romans 8:37–39

When Paul wrote to the Christians in Rome, early believers were trying to understand how to live faithfully. One of the issues they wrestled with was whether Gentile Christians should adopt the religious practices of Judaism. Paul writes a beautiful theological treatise that celebrates the Gospel of God's righteousness in Christ for all who believe. Again and again, Paul points to the sufficiency of Jesus to save. He also hammers home his confident belief that nothing can separate believers from Christ's love. Here his beautiful writing details all manner of calamity that might befall believers and then climaxes to confirm that nothing in all creation can separate us from the love God has for us in Christ. Today you are invited to borrow Paul's confidence and savor his certainty that we are held by God.

God, You know the kinds of troubles and dangers that threaten my faith today. Embolden me with the holy confidence that nothing can separate me from Your love. Amen.

Bind This Commandment to Your Heart

Hear, O Israel: The Lord *our God, the* Lord *is one. Love the* Lord *your God with all your heart and with all your soul and with all your strength. These commandments that I give you today are to be on your hearts.*
Deuteronomy 6:4–6

When Jesus was asked what the greatest commandment in the law was, He didn't hesitate. He answered immediately, "'Love the Lord your God with all your heart and with all your soul and with all your mind.' This is the first and greatest commandment" (Matthew 22:37–38). He was reiterating the command God gave to His people in Deuteronomy and giving it top billing. He let His followers know: this is *the most important thing*. The command God issued to Israel and the one Jesus gave to His followers was the same imperative that you and I have been charged with today. As you move throughout your day today, tomorrow, and this week, use it as a guide. At home, at work, at the grocery, you can quietly ask the Spirit to guide you as you purpose to love God with all of your heart, soul, and strength.

Lord God, You are One. Help me today to love You with all that I am. In every moment, show me what it means to love You with my heart, soul, and strength to Your glory. Amen.

You Have a Purpose as God's Image Bearer

Then God said, "Let us make mankind in our image, in our likeness, so that they may rule over the fish in the sea and the birds in the sky, over the livestock and all the wild animals, and over all the creatures that move along the ground."
Genesis 1:26

We have already agreed that, as someone who reflects God's image, you are altogether worthy. As someone who bears God's imprint, you are immeasurably valuable and precious to God. And along with the privilege of being God's own, you've also been given a responsibility as a coruler over the earth. Along with Adam and Eve, you've been given dominion to care for all that God has made. So, what will that mean for you today? As someone who is entirely worthy and who reflects God's image, how will you serve as the keeper of God's creation today? It may be in the way you choose to treat the earth or steward the resources God has entrusted to you. It might be in the way you care for animals or even for other people! Live today as someone called to care for all God has created.

God, I confess that my vision for who You've made me to be is often too small. I am reminded today that I bear Your image and I share in the work of ruling over Your world. Equip me to be Your faithful servant today. Amen.

Your Heavenly Father Cares for You

"Therefore I tell you, do not worry about your life, what you will eat or drink; or about your body, what you will wear. Is not life more than food, and the body more than clothes? Look at the birds of the air; they do not sow or reap or store away in barns, and yet your heavenly Father feeds them. Are you not much more valuable than they? Can any one of you by worrying add a single hour to your life?"

MATTHEW 6:25–27

Some of us spend a lot of time, energy, and money worrying about what we'll eat, what we'll drink, and what we'll wear. (Guilty!) And Jesus understands that, unchecked, this is our natural impulse. But because He wants us to live in freedom, He invites us to tip our eyes upward toward the birds of the air. He reminds us that they don't have bank accounts, credit cards, fridges, or closets, and our heavenly Father *still* feeds them. Is there a way today that God is inviting you to trust Him for what you most need? Are you being invited into the freedom of trusting God for what you need rather than scrambling after it yourself? Jesus confirms that you are so much more valuable than a bird of the sky and that your Father cares for you.

Father, I put my trust in You today. You are my good provider and I am counting on You to provide what I need. Thank You for meeting my needs and caring for me. Amen.

Though You No Longer Live, Christ Lives in You

"For through the law I died to the law so that I might live for God. I have been crucified with Christ and I no longer live, but Christ lives in me. The life I now live in the body, I live by faith in the Son of God, who loved me and gave himself for me. I do not set aside the grace of God, for if righteousness could be gained through the law, Christ died for nothing!"

Galatians 2:19–21

My son was baptized when he was two years old. His father was standing hip-deep in a nearby lake, and our church congregation was gathered at the water's edge. With our son wrapped tightly in his arms, I watched as his father dipped below the water and then burst back up, both of them gulping fresh air. That moment symbolized for my son, as it does for all of us, dying with Christ and being raised to new life with Him as well. When we join Jesus in His death, we also join Him in His resurrection from the grave. And when we rise after this death, leaving our old self behind, it is now Christ who is alive in us. We're free to love because now Christ is in us and loving through us. The life we live, we live *in Him*.

Jesus, I thank You that You are alive in me. Today, as I love those around me, I invite You to live through me and love through me. To Your glory, amen.

What's in Your Heart Comes Out Your Mouth

"A good man brings good things out of the good stored up in him, and an evil man brings evil things out of the evil stored up in him. But I tell you that everyone will have to give account on the day of judgment for every empty word they have spoken. For by your words you will be acquitted, and by your words you will be condemned."
MATTHEW 12:35–37

Have you ever noticed that something lodged in your heart usually finds its way out of your mouth? Maybe you're harboring a resentment at someone, and that private matter leaks out as gossip with another friend. Or maybe you are angry about something, and when you drop and break a coffee mug on the kitchen floor, you explode in ugly curse words that may or may not be related to the cheap mug you don't like or use. If you're like me, these leaks happen more often when I'm hungry, thirsty, or tired. And they serve to reveal what's *really* inside my heart. When you notice these leaks, learn from them. Offer them to God, and invite His Spirit to cleanse and heal your heart.

Father, You know my heart better than I do! Open my eyes to see any anger or ugliness I am harboring inside, and help me to release those to You. I long to be a vessel that holds and shares good things from You. Amen.

Living by God's Word

How can a young person stay on the path of purity? By living according to your word. I seek you with all my heart; do not let me stray from your commands. I have hidden your word in my heart that I might not sin against you.

PSALM 119:9–11

In a sexually permissive culture, purity has taken a bad rap the last few years. But there is a larger call to purity than one limited to sexuality. The psalmist names the young person's challenge to stay on the path of purity—a purity of heart, mind, and body. As someone who's no longer young, I'll be bold to say that this is a challenge for us all! And the psalmist points us toward the hope we have to live well. When we seek God with all our heart and trust in His Word, God helps keep us from straying from His commands. As we hide God's Word in our hearts—memorizing scripture, posting it on the bathroom mirror, and whispering it as we lie in bed—we are strengthened and equipped to stay on the path of purity.

Lord, You know that I long for my life to be a pleasing offering to You. I have heard Your call to the path of purity, and I commit myself to it today. Send Your Spirit to guide and strengthen me so that I might not sin against You. Amen.

God Is a Gracious Guest

"Those whom I love I rebuke and discipline. So be earnest and repent. Here I am! I stand at the door and knock. If anyone hears my voice and opens the door, I will come in and eat with that person, and they with me. To the one who is victorious, I will give the right to sit with me on my throne, just as I was victorious and sat down with my Father on his throne."

REVELATION 3:19–21

I've heard it said that God is a gentleman. The implication is that God does not force Himself into our lives where we have not welcomed Him to be. Maybe we've allowed God to shape the way we think about money, but we haven't been willing to invite God into our dating relationships. Or perhaps we've asked God to help us better love a relative who's difficult to love, but we haven't been willing to allow God to speak to us about forgiveness. The Lord is kind and gentle and waits outside the door to be welcomed in. Whenever we open that door and invite Him into our hearts to transform our lives, He is eager to be with us.

God, You know those areas of my life where I've not welcomed You. Forgive me. Today I offer You access to every part of me, and I welcome You to come into my life and transform my heart. Amen.

The Lord Will Not Turn Away When You Return to Him

"If you return to the Lord, then your fellow Israelites and your children will be shown compassion by their captors and will return to this land, for the Lord your God is gracious and compassionate. He will not turn his face from you if you return to him."
2 Chronicles 30:9

If you've known kids who've gotten in trouble for poor behavior, you know that their responses can range from overwhelming repentance to stubborn denial. And I suspect that grown-ups also find ourselves on that same spectrum after we've sinned! In scripture we hear a warm invitation to own up to what we've done, face it squarely, and return to the Lord. The promise is that when we are honest before God, good will come. Does it take courage? Yes. Does it take commitment? Absolutely. But we have the gracious assurance that when we return to God, He will not turn His face from us. Even when we've sinned, the Lord *receives us* when we return to Him. You might even imagine the beautiful snapshot of a wayward son returning home to a Father who runs to meet him, welcoming him with open arms. As you return to God, you can expect that same embrace.

Lord, forgive me for the ways I've strayed from Your way. Although I've sinned, I trust that You are gracious and compassionate. Receive me as I return to You. Amen.

I Come Against You in the Name of the Lord

David said to the Philistine, "You come against me with sword and spear and javelin, but I come against you in the name of the LORD Almighty, the God of the armies of Israel, whom you have defied."

1 SAMUEL 17:45

When the Philistines and the Israelites prepared to fight each other in a war, a nine-foot-tall Philistine giant named Goliath challenged Israel to send her fiercest champion to fight him. The winner would determine the outcome of the war and decide which nation would rule over the other. As you might imagine, no Israelite soldier was stepping forward! But when young David was sent by his father to take food to his brothers on the battlefield, David overheard Goliath's taunt and volunteered. Though King Saul tried to dissuade him, David was committed to fighting and winning. Vulnerable with no armor, David announced to the giant that he was fighting in the name of his God. And with a stone and a slingshot, small David defeated the giant. Who or what are the enemies in your life today? And is there a way that you are being called to trust God rather than to trust in weapons of war?

God, You know the enemies in my life I am struggling to defeat.
Today I put my trust in You, and I walk in Your unlikely way.
I believe that You will be my helper. In Your mighty name, amen.

A Gracious Provider Feeds Us

The Lord Jesus, on the night he was betrayed, took bread, and when he had given thanks, he broke it and said, "This is my body, which is for you; do this in remembrance of me." In the same way, after supper he took the cup, saying, "This cup is the new covenant in my blood; do this, whenever you drink it, in remembrance of me." For whenever you eat this bread and drink this cup, you proclaim the Lord's death until he comes.

1 Corinthians 11:23–26

As a well-fed American who eats very regularly—and often too frequently—each day I have a *limited experience of hunger*. But a recent health issue forced me to maintain a very restricted diet I would never have chosen for myself. Truly, because the foods I eat every day do not satisfy my big, very active body, I am *usually* hungry. Because I have easy access to all the food I need, I still don't know what it is to be poor and hungry. But I do know for certain, in my *cells*, that we need to be fed! We need fuel to flourish. And on the night He was betrayed, Jesus helped His followers understand that He was giving them *Himself*. Although they couldn't understand His sacrifice in that moment, they eventually came not only to understand but to be nourished and fed by the life of Jesus.

Lord, Your sacrifice for us is a mystery! But I do believe that You are the Bread of Life that I need to flourish and thrive. Feed me with Your body and blood. Amen.

This Is Where You Find Rest for Your Souls

"Come to me, all you who are weary and burdened, and I will give you rest. Take my yoke upon you and learn from me, for I am gentle and humble in heart, and you will find rest for your souls. For my yoke is easy and my burden is light."
MATTHEW 11:28–30

Back in the day there was a myth floating around that if you gave your life to Jesus, if you offered Him your whole heart, He would send you overseas as a missionary to unreached peoples. While that's an adventure in obedience for those who actually are called to overseas mission work, it was pretty terrifying for the rest of us! Our fear was that if we gave our entire lives to the Lord, we would lose them. While Jesus does transform our lives, He is always concerned with our good.

Matthew reports an invitation from Jesus that invites weary and burdened people to find rest in Him. Yes, there is a yoke to be carried, but Jesus assures us that the yoke He gives us is easy and His burden is light. Beloved, Jesus can be trusted with your whole heart and your whole life. As you approach Him, as you spend time in His presence, may you be refreshed by rest and may you discover His gentleness.

Jesus, I am weary, and I believe that You are calling me to discover rest in You. Teach me Your ways and refresh my soul. Amen.

Be Still and Know That I Am God

He says, "Be still, and know that I am God; I will be exalted among the nations, I will be exalted in the earth." The Lord *Almighty is with us; the God of Jacob is our fortress.*

Psalm 46:10–11

A lot of us have swallowed the lie that we should be *busy*. Though we may be hesitant to admit it, we've believed the lie that our worth is somehow found in what we achieve, so we overcommit ourselves at church, school, and work. We dutifully attend our children's sports, neighbor's theater performances, and colleague's concerts. Then we race around like chickens with our heads cut off to accomplish the long list of tasks and shopping errands that never seem to get finished. In the midst of our madness, we hear a gentle voice summoning, "Be still." *Be still? But nothing will get done if I am still.* Exactly. This kind invitation is a practical way to acknowledge that God is God and we are not. When we practice stillness in God's presence, we agree to that undeniable reality. Carve out time to be still today: no screens, no gadgets, no *anything*. Give yourself the radically countercultural gift of being still in God's presence.

God, You know my heart, and You know all the reasons that my life can feel frantic at times. I receive Your gracious invitation to stillness, and I welcome You to abide with me as I choose to be still. Amen.

God Heard, Saw, Knew, and Cared

God heard their groaning and he remembered his covenant with Abraham, with Isaac and with Jacob. So God looked on the Israelites and was concerned about them.

EXODUS 2:24–25

The Hebrew people were enslaved in Egypt for as many as four hundred years. It's hard to imagine, isn't it? As God's people suffered under cruel taskmasters, they cried out to Him for help. I imagine that many assumed God had abandoned them, but Exodus says that those cries ascended to God's ears. We discover in Exodus that when God heard the groaning of the people He loved, He remembered His covenant with Abraham, Isaac, and Jacob. He saw their suffering and was concerned about them. In a mighty act of redemption, God used Moses to part the sea through which His people were delivered out of bondage. This is *who God is*. It is who God was for the Hebrew people, and it is who God is for us today. God hears your cries. God sees your tears. God notices. And cares.

Lord, I trust that You have heard the desperate cries of my heart. You know where I hurt, and I believe that You care. God, I am waiting for Your redemption. I am counting on You to be my deliverer so that You might be glorified. Amen.

We Worship the One Who Calms the Storm

Then he got into the boat and his disciples followed him. Suddenly a furious storm came up on the lake, so that the waves swept over the boat. But Jesus was sleeping. The disciples went and woke him, saying, "Lord, save us! We're going to drown!" He replied, "You of little faith, why are you so afraid?" Then he got up and rebuked the winds and the waves, and it was completely calm.

MATTHEW 8:23–26

If you've ever been on a boat in a storm, you know how precarious it can feel. Not only are you being pelted by the winds and the rains, but the waves are also violently shifting beneath you. So, when a furious storm came up on the lake—with huge waves *sweeping over the boat*—it was fairly reasonable that the disciples would be afraid! And that was why Jesus' response to them was so surprising. He called them out for being scared, even labeling it a lack of faith. Jesus expected His closest friends to have confidence in who He was. In this moment, you and I are privy to witness His power firsthand. How is Jesus inviting you to trust Him today? What fear is He welcoming you to relinquish into His care?

Jesus, too often I am just like Your first disciples: quick to fear and slow to believe. Help me to trust that You are the Lord of heaven and earth, and even the winds and the waves submit to You. Amen.

Come, Let Us Sing for Joy to the Lord

Come, let us sing for joy to the LORD; let us shout aloud to the Rock of our salvation. Let us come before him with thanksgiving and extol him with music and song. For the LORD is the great God, the great King above all gods.

PSALM 95:1–3

If you're like me, you might be tempted to save worshipping God in song for Sunday mornings. When the keyboards are jumping and the bass is thumping, I love to rock and sway and worship God with my body and voice. But Monday? Thursday? I'm more likely to be dancing to a Stevie Wonder song or singing backups for Beyoncé. But I recently began to notice that my heart *needed* to connect with God in worship during the week. I yearned to experience God's presence in the rhythm of my everyday life. So, I began to use a playlist I created for the purpose of connecting with and worshipping God. Now when my soul feels fragmented or my heart feels heavy, I can shout aloud to the Rock of my salvation, extolling Him with music and song.

Lord, You are the great God, the great King above all gods, and You are worthy to be praised. I offer You my heart and body and voice as I praise and worship You. Thank You for being the Rock of my salvation. Amen.

What You Did for Jesus

"Then the righteous will answer him, 'Lord, when did we see you hungry and feed you, or thirsty and give you something to drink? When did we see you a stranger and invite you in, or needing clothes and clothe you? When did we see you sick or in prison and go to visit you?' The King will reply, 'Truly I tell you, whatever you did for one of the least of these brothers and sisters of mine, you did for me.' "

MATTHEW 25:37–40

Precious one, I pray that you are discovering and believing in your deep places that you are worthy of God's loving care. You are. I am. We are. And the beautiful flip side of that undeniable reality is that those around us—both those we've deemed worthy and those we've not—are also worthy of God's love. In Jesus' culture and in ours, folks on the margins have often been considered unworthy. In the ancient world in particular, it was believed that misfortune was brought about by a person's sin. Yet Jesus confirmed that those on the margins—the hungry, the thirsty, the stranger, the naked, the sick, the imprisoned—were entirely worthy of care. It's not just that they're as precious as you or I; He insists that when you love them, you are actually loving *Him*.

Jesus, open my eyes. Show me the folks in my orbit who are in need, and quicken my heart to respond to them the way I would respond to You. Be my helper, for the sake of Your kingdom. Amen.

Taste and See That the Lord Is Good

Taste and see that the Lord *is good; blessed is the one who takes refuge in him. Fear the* Lord*, you his holy people, for those who fear him lack nothing. The lions may grow weak and hungry, but those who seek the* Lord *lack no good thing.*

Psalm 34:8–10

When my son was small, I pitched him the idea that delicious strawberries, grapes, blueberries, and watermelon were kind of like God's *candy*. He hadn't been paying much attention, but when he heard the word *candy*, he perked right up, asking, "What's dat about Dod's CANDY?" When they are ripe, sweet juicy fruits can be the most delicious treat under the sun (barring candy, of course). And the psalmist is welcoming the people of God not just to know "about" God—the way we'd know if a fruit was red, green, blue, or pink—but to *experience* God firsthand. The psalmist welcomes us to encounter God for ourselves as the One who is our protector and provider who gives us all that we need.

God, I long for a deeper experience of You. I know lots of information about You, but I long to taste and know and experience You firsthand. In our time together, let me encounter You for myself today! Amen.

Whatever Is Good, Think about Such Things

Finally, brothers and sisters, whatever is true, whatever is noble, whatever is right, whatever is pure, whatever is lovely, whatever is admirable—if anything is excellent or praiseworthy—think about such things. Whatever you have learned or received or heard from me, or seen in me—put it into practice. And the God of peace will be with you.

Philippians 4:8–9

In Paul's greeting to the church at Philippi, he encouraged them to put their trust in God, who would guard their hearts and minds in Christ Jesus. And here he continued to name the *good* that should be occupying their minds. He implored them to focus on what was true. To concentrate on what was noble rather than what was degrading. To think about what was right rather than what was wrong. To meditate on what was pure rather than that which was filthy. To noodle on what was lovely rather than that which was ugly. To aspire to what was admirable rather than what was shameful. He begged them to set their minds on anything that was excellent or praiseworthy. How do you receive Paul's encouragement today? Is there a place where you've let what is unholy occupy your thoughts? Count this your opportunity to offer that to the Lord, and replace it with what is best.

Lord, You know my mind perhaps better than I do! Send Your Holy Spirit to quicken my thoughts so I might catch the ways that my mind goes astray. Fill me with Your beauty and truth! Amen.

I Will Walk among You

"I will look on you with favor and make you fruitful and increase your numbers, and I will keep my covenant with you. You will still be eating last year's harvest when you will have to move it out to make room for the new. I will put my dwelling place among you, and I will not abhor you. I will walk among you and be your God, and you will be my people."

Leviticus 26:9–12

For cultures and civilizations throughout the ages, "god" and "gods" have been a pretty wily concept to grasp with our human senses! But the God who created the universe chose to enter human history, making Himself known to Abraham, Isaac, and Jacob. He rescued His people from bondage in Egypt and led them to a land of milk and honey. And at just the right time, this God of love chose to take on human flesh to be among us. He promised His presence when He gave the law and entered covenant with His people, and He fulfilled that covenant through the flesh-and-blood person of Jesus Christ. Graciously, we had a God who walked among us and knew what our lives were like. We still do.

Lord, I thank You that You chose to come near. Although You are the Lord of the universe, You are not distant and remote. By Your Holy Spirit, You are as close as the air we breathe. Thank You for choosing to walk among us and be our God. Amen.

There Shall Be One Flock and One Shepherd

"I am the good shepherd; I know my sheep and my sheep know me—just as the Father knows me and I know the Father—and I lay down my life for the sheep. I have other sheep that are not of this sheep pen. I must bring them also. They too will listen to my voice, and there shall be one flock and one shepherd."

John 10:14–16

Those of us who have lived in the twentieth and twenty-first centuries have an experience of the Church of Jesus Christ that is very different from the one that blossomed in the first century. A body of Christ that has been splintered throughout history is our only experience of Church. If we're Baptist, then we're *not* Lutheran. If we're Wesleyans, we're *not* Calvinists. If we're Protestants, then we're *not* Roman Catholics. If we're Roman Catholics, we're *not* Greek Orthodox. If we're Gentile believers, we're *not* Messianic believers. For the best of reasons and the worst of reasons, the Church of Jesus has been fractured over the centuries. But from Jesus' own lips, we discover that His heart for His Church is that we would be one. How can you live into that unity today? How can you delight the heart of Jesus by embodying the oneness of His Church?

Jesus, You made Yourself known to us as the Good Shepherd, and we believe that You long for Your flock to be one. I pray for Your Church, that we might function as the singular body You intended for our life together. Amen.

He Turned and Heard My Cry

I waited patiently for the Lord; he turned to me and heard my cry.
He lifted me out of the slimy pit, out of the mud and mire;
he set my feet on a rock and gave me a firm place to stand.
Psalm 40:1–2

When your feet are in the slimy pit, it can be hard to believe in a Savior who is poised to rescue you. And if you must *wait* on that Savior as you cry out for mercy, the wait can feel absolutely agonizing. But when you wait and believe in the perfect timing of a good Savior, you exercise your spiritual muscles. You grow as you rehearse your confidence in God's goodness over time. But the Lord knows that waiting is hard. Are your feet in the pit today? Are they sticky with mud? You can be confident that your Savior is on the way. And when He rescues you, He pulls you out of the pit and sets you on solid ground. He actually becomes the Rock on whom you can build your life. If you're waiting today, continue to cry out to your Savior for mercy. Help is on the way.

Lord, I am waiting for Your rescue. I am weary and I am stuck. I cry out to You as my deliverer, and I wait for Your redemption. No matter what my circumstances are today, I put my trust in You. Amen.

The Kind of Fast God Has Chosen

"Is not this the kind of fasting I have chosen: to loose the chains of injustice and untie the cords of the yoke, to set the oppressed free and break every yoke? Is it not to share your food with the hungry and to provide the poor wanderer with shelter—when you see the naked, to clothe them, and not to turn away from your own flesh and blood?"

Isaiah 58:6–7

God's ancient people were accustomed to the holy rhythm and ritual of prayer and fasting. But the Lord began to notice that those who checked the box on practicing the rituals of religion were mistreating the people who were working for them. So God spoke through the prophet Isaiah to announce the kind of fast that moved His heart. It would be a fast in which the chains of injustice were loosed. It showed itself as the oppressed being set free, breaking every yoke. It could be seen when His people shared their food with those who were hungry and offered shelter to poor wanderers. Or clothing the naked and caring for their families. In the ancient world and in the modern one, this is the kind of fasting that delights God's heart.

God, I confess that I am tempted to blame mistreatment on others: on CEOs or factory managers or slave holders. But I know that's too easy. So, open my eyes to the ways I participate in the mistreatment of others, and teach me how to honor You with a fast that reflects Your love for the world. Amen.

Doing Everything in Love

Be on your guard; stand firm in the faith;
be courageous; be strong. Do everything in love.
1 CORINTHIANS 16:13–14

Because life can feel overwhelming sometimes—the bills, groceries, laundry, family commitments, committees, car inspections, and plumbing repairs—it can also feel overwhelming to commit to living well. As followers of Jesus, we were made to pattern our lives after His. But living that out in our homes, jobs, schools, churches, and communities can potentially feel like *one more thing to do*. Except that it's not. As Jesus was completing His earthly ministry, we overhear Him giving a pretty clear prime directive to His closest followers: *love*. Love one another. And as we listen in on Paul's exhortation to the early believers in Corinth, we hear that same instruction: *do everything in love*. So, when the alarm clock goes off in the morning and our feet hit the ground running, we don't have to add anything special to what we're doing. No, the call is actually to live our lives—at home, work, school, church, community—in a fresh way: *in love*. As you purpose today to do everything in love, what will look different in your encounters with others?

Lord, I believe that You have made me for life. You've also promised that Your yoke is easy and Your burden is light. Today I welcome You to live in me and through me as I encounter others. Teach me what it looks like to do everything in love to Your glory. Amen.

Because You Are Precious and Honored in My Sight

"For I am the LORD your God, the Holy One of Israel, your Savior; I give Egypt for your ransom, Cush and Seba in your stead. Since you are precious and honored in my sight, and because I love you, I will give people in exchange for you, nations in exchange for your life. Do not be afraid, for I am with you; I will bring your children from the east and gather you from the west."

ISAIAH 43:3–5

Many scholars believe that much of the book of Isaiah, the first of the major prophets in the Old Testament, was written during the Babylonian captivity. In the second of three parts of the book, God spoke through the prophet to bring comfort to God's people who were being held as captives in Babylonia. As we listen to God's message of hope to those who suffer, we hear strains of hope for our own lives as well. God announces who He is as a holy God and Savior, One who is willing to pay a high ransom to free His people. He comforts and nurtures them by assuring them that they are precious and honored and loved by Him. And He promises His presence with them. As you face challenges this week, know that you are being held by God's power, God's love, and God's presence.

God, I thank You that You've revealed who You are through the scriptures. Today I put my confidence in Your power as a Savior, in Your steadfast love, and in Your presence with me in every moment. Amen.

Every Good and Perfect Gift Is from Above

Don't be deceived, my dear brothers and sisters. Every good and perfect gift is from above, coming down from the Father of the heavenly lights, who does not change like shifting shadows. He chose to give us birth through the word of truth, that we might be a kind of firstfruits of all he created.

JAMES 1:16–18

If we had the privilege of attending college or graduate school, we might pat ourselves on the back for our hard work. Or if we hustled to achieve career success, we might quietly believe that we have earned everything that has come our way. If we were fortunate enough to find a loving spouse or birth the right number of children, it can be tempting to believe that we are somehow responsible for the gifts we've experienced. When we notice the blessings in our lives, it can be easy to deceive ourselves. But James cautions us to note where these gifts are from, insisting that every good and perfect gift from above is from the Father who loves us. As you practice gratitude for the good in your life, thank the One who is the giver of all good gifts.

Lord, forgive me for neglecting to give You thanks and praise for all of Your rich blessings that I enjoy. I acknowledge You as the giver of all that is good. Teach me to practice gratitude to You for all that You have given. Amen.

If You Want to See the Father. . .

Philip said, "Lord, show us the Father and that will be enough for us." Jesus answered: "Don't you know me, Philip, even after I have been among you such a long time? Anyone who has seen me has seen the Father. How can you say, 'Show us the Father'? Don't you believe that I am in the Father, and that the Father is in me?"

John 14:8–10

Boy, when I read John's retelling of a conversation between Jesus and His disciples, I *really* feel for Philip. It is the end of Jesus' earthly ministry, and He is preparing His followers for His departure. He's just announced to them that if they know Him, they know His Father as well. Poor Philip is just not getting it yet. (And, to be fair, I don't think that you or I could have understood Jesus' words either!) Jesus gently rebukes Philip, asking, "Don't you believe that I am in the Father, and that the Father is in me?" This holy mystery that has baffled theologians for centuries had just unfolded in front of the disciples' eyes: the Father of Jesus had been present with them—in the flesh! So today we have the confidence that we can see, hear, and know Him intimately through the person of Jesus.

God, open my eyes to see Your face. As I discover Jesus in the scriptures, let me know more and more of Your character and Your love for me. Thank You for loving us so much that You have made Yourself known. Amen.

What Can Mere Mortals Do to Me?

When I am afraid, I put my trust in you. In God, whose word I praise—in God I trust and am not afraid. What can mere mortals do to me?
Psalm 56:3–4

In 1563, Reformed Christians gathered in present-day Germany to create a catechism, a condensed teaching as a series of questions and answers, of what they believed. This confession of faith continues to guide the life of the Church today. In answer to the first question, "What is your only comfort in life and in death?" the Christian response is "That I am not my own, but belong with body and soul, both in life and in death, to my faithful Saviour Jesus Christ." In it I hear echoes of Romans 8:38, in which Paul insists that neither death nor life can separate us from God's love. And we also hear this beautiful refrain from the psalmist who asks, "What can mere mortals do to me?" First the psalmist and then Paul and eventually Christians who lived centuries later all agree that when we trust in God, we need not fear either the wiles of man or the power of the grave. In life and in death, we belong to God!

Lord, when I am afraid, I put my trust in You. Because of who You are, I trust and am not afraid. Thank You for the confidence I receive from Your Word that I am held in Your loving care in life and in death. Amen.

You Have Already Been Set Free

But now that you have been set free from sin and have become slaves of God, the benefit you reap leads to holiness, and the result is eternal life. For the wages of sin is death, but the gift of God is eternal life in Christ Jesus our Lord.
Romans 6:22–23

At the end of a long, hard week, Laura reaches for a bottle of wine and drinks until she doesn't remember what happened that week. Joanne, also hungry to be filled, heads to the mall and charges purchases on her credit card she knows she doesn't have the money to pay for. And Sarah's drug of choice is Netflix and the couch, where she can spend countless hours numbing herself from feeling the hurts in her heart. Graciously, Paul's message to the church in Rome speaks to the ways we continue to be stuck in sin. He reminds believers, "You have been set free from sin and have become slaves of God." Practically, that means we no longer have to live in bondage to patterns of sin and death in our lives. Will freedom require something from us? Yes. Will God give us the strength to choose life that really is life? Absolutely. Notice where you are stuck in ruts of sin and death, and ask God to be your helper today.

Lord, You know how stuck I am. But I believe that Jesus has set me free from the power of sin and death and that You empower me by Your Spirit to live as a free woman. Amen.

Let Us Love Like Jesus Loved

This is how we know what love is: Jesus Christ laid down his life for us. And we ought to lay down our lives for our brothers and sisters. If anyone has material possessions and sees a brother or sister in need but has no pity on them, how can the love of God be in that person? Dear children, let us not love with words or speech but with actions and in truth.

1 John 3:16–18

There is a lot out there these days that masquerades as love. A teenage boy pressures his girlfriend to sleep with him if she loves him. A woman confronts a friend with ugly, unkind words in the name of love. And an abusive partner tries to convince the fiancée he's abused that he loves her. In the end, it almost feels as if love is a matter of opinion! But we have been given a guide to know what love is: Jesus Christ laid down His life for us. Having been loved perfectly by Christ, we are invited to lay down our own lives for our brothers and sisters. To serve them with our gifts. To share our resources. To love them sacrificially like Jesus has loved us. And we're reminded that what we say really doesn't matter as much as what we *do*.

Lord Jesus, You have demonstrated perfect love by laying Your life down for me. Guide me today as I purpose to love those around me the way You have loved me. May You be glorified. Amen.

Lean Not on Your Own Understanding

Let love and faithfulness never leave you; bind them around your neck, write them on the tablet of your heart. Then you will win favor and a good name in the sight of God and man. Trust in the LORD with all your heart and lean not on your own understanding; in all your ways submit to him, and he will make your paths straight.

PROVERBS 3:3–6

When I notice the lives of the people I love, there's an awful lot I don't understand. I don't understand why my friend Sloan is so limited by his physical disability and painful suffering. I don't understand why Tricia hasn't found a partner with whom to share her life. I don't understand why many of my friends who are financially poor are afflicted by so many challenges and never seem to catch a break. With my own reasoning, I can't make sense of much of what I see around me. The psalmist understood the limits of my human reasoning. And he exhorts, "Trust in the LORD with all your heart and lean not on your own understanding." Though I don't have an explanation or reason for what I see in the lives of others or even for the way my own life has unfolded, I am being invited to trust a higher reason. You are too.

Lord, I confess that I do not understand Your ways, so I relinquish my dependence on my own understanding as I purpose to trust You. Amen.

God Sent Jesus for This

Unrolling it, he found the place where it is written: "The Spirit of the Lord is on me, because he has anointed me to proclaim good news to the poor. He has sent me to proclaim freedom for the prisoners and recovery of sight for the blind, to set the oppressed free, to proclaim the year of the Lord's favor."

Luke 4:17–19

Scholars suggest that Jesus was about thirty years old when He began His public ministry. In Luke's Gospel, we get to witness, along with Jesus' community, how that ministry began. He'd gone to the synagogue in His hometown of Nazareth on the Sabbath. When He stood to read, He was handed the scroll of the prophet Isaiah. If Jesus had been an elected official, this would have been His inaugural address. Reading the words written centuries earlier, foretelling the Savior God would send, Jesus spoke, "The Spirit of the Lord is on me, because he has anointed me." He then continued to announce the initiatives He'd champion during His time in office. Because the Jews had been waiting for the One God would send, Jesus had made a *radical* announcement! And yet as we follow His ministry throughout the Gospels, we see Him doing exactly what Isaiah had prophesied God's servant would do.

Jesus, thank You that You proclaimed good news to the poor, freedom for the captives, and recovery of sight for the blind. You set the oppressed free and You announced good news. Today, equip me to partner in the work of building the kingdom You ushered in. Amen.

Do Not Worry about Tomorrow

"But seek first his kingdom and his righteousness, and all these things will be given to you as well. Therefore do not worry about tomorrow, for tomorrow will worry about itself. Each day has enough trouble of its own."
MATTHEW 6:33–34

Left to our own devices, we worry about tomorrow. We try to put away money for retirement. We save for the needs of our families that we can anticipate. We buy lots of toilet paper so that we don't run out. And if we're particularly efficient, we might even prep meals on Sunday to last through the week. When Jesus spoke to crowds on a mountainside, He knew that this is how we operate. We scramble to ensure that our needs will be met. But He offered a beautiful alternate possibility: "Do not worry about tomorrow, for tomorrow will worry about itself." And He suggested that when we seek God's kingdom and righteousness *first*, the rest of what we need will be given to us. That is a pretty radical upside-down economy! This week, trust that God will meet your needs.

Father, You know that I am wired to think and worry about tomorrow. But I believe that You are faithful. As I set my mind on Your kingdom, I trust that You are providing what I need. Amen.

When I Am Weak, Then I Am Strong

But he said to me, "My grace is sufficient for you, for my power is made perfect in weakness." Therefore I will boast all the more gladly about my weaknesses, so that Christ's power may rest on me. That is why, for Christ's sake, I delight in weaknesses, in insults, in hardships, in persecutions, in difficulties. For when I am weak, then I am strong.

2 Corinthians 12:9–10

Given our druthers, we would rather be rich than poor. We'd choose health over sickness. We'd avoid pain rather than embrace it. We'd prefer to be happy instead of sad. And if we had a choice, we'd opt for power over weakness. Because we've been naturally wired to pursue comfort and pleasure, left unchecked, this is how human beings operate. But a God who took on human flesh chose to use frail human vessels to reach the world He loves, because God's power is on display in those who are weak. Like water running through a broken vessel, giving life to others, God has chosen to use our weaknesses to display His power. So, when your weakness is exposed, offer it to God.

Lord, You know that I wouldn't choose some of the weaknesses, insults, hardships, persecutions, or difficulties I've faced. But I do believe Your Word and trust that Your strength is made known through my weakness. Fill me with Your power today. Amen.

He Binds Up the Brokenhearted

The Spirit of the Sovereign Lord is on me, because the Lord has anointed me to proclaim good news to the poor. He has sent me to bind up the brokenhearted, to proclaim freedom for the captives and release from darkness for the prisoners, to proclaim the year of the Lord's favor and the day of vengeance of our God, to comfort all who mourn, and provide for those who grieve in Zion.

Isaiah 61:1–3

When God's people were suffering in exile, He sent the prophet Isaiah to speak His true words to their hearts. And to this aching people God foretold the One who would someday redeem all those who trusted in Him. The suffering servant that Isaiah described would redeem those who were bound by poverty and chains and prison gates. But God also promised to minister to the hurting *hearts* of those who had been oppressed, assuring His people that the One to come would "bind up the brokenhearted." And we have witnessed the realization of Isaiah's prophecy in the person of Jesus. When He wept with Lazarus's sisters, when He raised a sick girl, and when He received a scorned woman, He cared for the *hearts* of those who suffered.

Father, You know the ways that my heart has been bruised and broken. With confidence that You bind up broken hearts, I offer You mine today. I trust You as a good healer. Amen.

If You've Seen Jesus, You've Seen the Father

Thomas said to him, "Lord, we don't know where you are going, so how can we know the way?" Jesus answered, "I am the way and the truth and the life. No one comes to the Father except through me. If you really know me, you will know my Father as well. From now on, you do know him and have seen him."

John 14:5–7

In the Old Testament, knowing that no one could look on the face of God and live, God's people practiced reverence for a mighty and holy God. God could be known through His commandments, prophets, priests, and kings. And God's holy presence was made manifest among His people in a burning bush, a pillar of fire, or a cloud of smoke. But God's people wouldn't have presumed to look upon God's face; so when God took on flesh in the person of Jesus, no one had a category for being able to lay eyes on God. At the end of Jesus' earthly ministry, Jesus revealed to His friends, "If you really know me, you will know my Father as well. From now on, you do know him and have seen him." Today—with the gift of theological hindsight!—we have the gift of "seeing" the Father's face when we get to know Jesus.

Father, I thank You that You long to be known! And thank You for the gift of Your Word through which I can know Jesus. Open my eyes to see Your face and my ears to hear Your voice. Amen.

Pray for Those in Power

I urge, then, first of all, that petitions, prayers, intercession and thanksgiving be made for all people—for kings and all those in authority, that we may live peaceful and quiet lives in all godliness and holiness. This is good, and pleases God our Savior, who wants all people to be saved and to come to a knowledge of the truth.

1 Timothy 2:1–4

This week I received an email from a woman I know who has a heart for those who are oppressed. Currently, she is particularly concerned about one of the pressing social and political issues of the day. (Use your imagination and choose the issue that most lights a fire in your heart!) This godly woman was appealing to her friends and fans to pray for a particular person who's involved with the issue in news headlines. And because I didn't recognize his name, I assumed that he was someone who was suffering as a result of the government's current policies. But as I read her request, I realized that the man she wanted us to pray for wasn't someone who was oppressed. No, he was actually a government official who is instrumental in shaping and executing the policies! And although I was surprised, her request was a holy one. God calls us to pray for those in authority when we agree with them and when we don't.

Lord, I appeal to You as the highest authority to let justice roll down like waters. Send Your Spirit to convict and guide the hearts and minds of those in authority so that Your kingdom might come on earth as it is in heaven. For Your glory, amen.

The Word of God Is Alive

For the word of God is alive and active. Sharper than any double-edged sword, it penetrates even to dividing soul and spirit, joints and marrow; it judges the thoughts and attitudes of the heart. Nothing in all creation is hidden from God's sight. Everything is uncovered and laid bare before the eyes of him to whom we must give account.

Hebrews 4:12–13

The opinion of some is that the Bible is an ancient text without relevance to modern life. They dismiss it as a product of a foreign culture, written centuries ago, with antiquated notions about God and humanity. But those who have tasted God's goodness and whose hearts have been vivified by God's Spirit experience something very different when we encounter God in His Holy Word. In scripture, we experience words that are actually alive and active. These living words have the power to penetrate our souls, our minds, our hearts. They uncover what we try to hide, exposing who we are. We can see what God sees in us—because of God's living Word! Beloved, access the gift of God's Word this week, and allow it to work in your heart and mind for God's glory and for your flourishing.

Father, I thank You that Your Word is alive and active. I submit myself to You, and I listen for what You are speaking to me through Your Word. Use it to reveal what is inside me, that I might glorify You with my life. Amen.

You Have Worth Because He Is Worthy

"You are worthy, our Lord and God, to receive glory and honor and power, for you created all things, and by your will they were created and have their being."
REVELATION 4:11

A neighbor of mine is a potter. He made a beautiful set of bowls, etched in creative designs and glazed in earth tones, that my family uses every day. Every bowl is different, and yet each one reflects something of the potter who formed it. In fact, they're beautiful *because* of the one who made them. And you are as well. Too often we try to discern our worth by looking sideways at other people. We glance at the other bowls on the shelf to decide if we have more or less value than they do. Ultimately, we're left anxiously wondering. The only way to know our true worth is to tip our faces up to the One who made us. Only when we notice the character of God, when we know who He is, can we discover the immutable worth He has bestowed on each one of us. Beloved, you are precious and worthy because you have been shaped and formed by a mighty Creator.

God, You are worthy to receive glory and honor and power. You are a good Creator who made all things. Because I have been formed by Your hand, You have deemed me worthy. I thank You for that blessed assurance in the strong name of Jesus. Amen.

You Are a Dearly Loved Child

Follow God's example, therefore, as dearly loved children and walk in the way of love, just as Christ loved us and gave himself up for us as a fragrant offering and sacrifice to God.

EPHESIANS 5:1–2

Yesterday I ran into a friend who is the mother of an eleven-month-old baby. We remembered together that before she and her husband conceived, we were praying for the child God would bring them. Today Gina *glows* when she speaks about her daughter. She adores this girl's joy, her laugh, and her spirit. And when I heard the way Gina cherishes her girl, I was reminded of the unbridled love God has for you and for me. In a little letter to the church in Ephesus, Paul reminds the believers that they are "dearly loved" children. And because they're dearly loved, he exhorts them to walk in the way of love just as Christ loved them. He reminds them that Christ's love is sacrificial. In the same way Jesus gave His life for us, we're invited to give our lives for others. As daughters who are "dearly loved," it is what we were made for!

Father, thank You for Your tender, steadfast love for me. Make me a vessel of Your love and quicken my heart to love others the way Christ loved me. Give me courage to sacrifice because I belong to You. Amen.

Be Filled with the Spirit

Therefore do not be foolish, but understand what the Lord's will is. Do not get drunk on wine, which leads to debauchery. Instead, be filled with the Spirit, speaking to one another with psalms, hymns, and songs from the Spirit. Sing and make music from your heart to the Lord, always giving thanks to God the Father for everything, in the name of our Lord Jesus Christ.

EPHESIANS 5:17–20

Jesus announced that He came so we could have life and have it to the full (John 10:10). And God designed us to *be full*. But too often we fill ourselves with things that fail to satisfy. In different seasons of my life, I have used delicious foods, caffeinated beverages, binging on entertainment, and even spending money to try to *fill* myself. Others try alcohol, pills, pornography, and even relationships to try to fill what feels like a gnawing void inside. But when he writes to the church in Ephesus, Paul exhorts them to avoid the kinds of fillers that fail—like getting drunk on wine—and instead to be filled by the Spirit. This is what we were *made for*! And I suspect that the practices he suggests—speaking and singing songs from God's Word and from His Spirit and giving thanks—help us to *remain filled* with God's Spirit.

God, You know the places inside where I am empty. And You know how I thirst for Your Spirit. Fill me today with the presence, comfort, and power of Your Holy Spirit. Amen.

Your Light Will Break Forth

"Then your light will break forth like the dawn, and your healing will quickly appear; then your righteousness will go before you, and the glory of the Lord will be your rear guard. Then you will call, and the Lord will answer; you will cry for help, and he will say: Here am I."

Isaiah 58:8–9

From Oprah to Doctor Phil to Brené Brown to Doctor Oz, there are countless voices who are offering us a path to health and happiness and fulfillment. And not all of them are bad paths! But in Isaiah's prophecy to a wayward and sinful people, God offers a pretty surprising road map to health and wholeness. God has just instructed His people to pursue justice, to share their food with the hungry, to clothe the naked, and to offer shelter to the wanderer. And God promises that when you do, "Your light will break forth like the dawn, and your healing will quickly appear." He continues to say that when we execute justice and mercy, He hears our cries and blesses us with His presence. It's a surprising formula for success, isn't it? Instead of pursuing our own ends, we are to seek the good of the most vulnerable. Then we will be blessed!

Lord, the way to joy and healing and wellness that You lay out is surprising and countercultural! God, make me an instrument of justice in the lives of those You love who lie on the world's margins. Equip me to loose the chains of injustice and set the oppressed free for the glory of Your name. Amen.

Prayer That Delights the Father

"And when you pray, do not be like the hypocrites, for they love to pray standing in the synagogues and on the street corners to be seen by others. Truly I tell you, they have received their reward in full. But when you pray, go into your room, close the door and pray to your Father, who is unseen. Then your Father, who sees what is done in secret, will reward you."

MATTHEW 6:5–6

The world insists we should store up riches for ourselves, and Jesus coaches us to give away what we have. The world insists that we should accrue an impressive home, and Jesus charges us to practice radical hospitality by welcoming the poor. The world bullies us into believing that how we look on the outside is what matters most, but scripture reveals that God looks on the heart. The radical Gospel inversion of the world's values is even true of our spiritual lives! "Religion" would have us praying loudly where we can be seen, using as many words as possible. But in His Sermon on the Mount, Jesus challenges His followers to pray in secret. When you pray in secret, He says, your Father will reward you. This week, carve out secret time with the Father who loves you.

Lord, I thank You that You listen to my prayers and You know what I need before I ask. You are a faithful Father and my good Provider. Amen.

You Do Not Lack Any Spiritual Gift

I always thank my God for you because of his grace given you in Christ Jesus. For in him you have been enriched in every way—with all kinds of speech and with all knowledge—God thus confirming our testimony about Christ among you. Therefore you do not lack any spiritual gift as you eagerly wait for our Lord Jesus Christ to be revealed.
1 Corinthians 1:4–7

In the first century after Jesus' death, resurrection, and ascension, believers were discovering what it meant to live as His followers in the season after His death and before His ultimate return. They believed, as we do, that Jesus Christ would return to earth, but they didn't know how long that period of time would be. (I don't think they were anticipating more than twenty centuries!) And Paul wrote to the believers in the church in Corinth to encourage them in that season. What he most wanted them to hear was that there was nothing they needed for that journey that they *lacked*. They had been equipped with every spiritual gift that they needed to stand firm until the day when Jesus returned. And his words remain true today: you and I have been equipped with all that we need to *stand firm*. What is it that you need God to provide today?

Father, I thank You for the hope and assurance that Jesus will return to earth, and I long to remain faithful until that day. Equip me with all I need to stand firm and glorify You. Amen.

Give Me a Sign of Your Goodness

Give me a sign of your goodness, that my enemies may see it and be put to shame, for you, Lord, have helped me and comforted me.
Psalm 86:17

In the darkest and most difficult seasons of my journey, it has been hard to recognize God's love and kindness. As God was healing some of the hurts I endured in childhood, I wasn't yet convinced that God was *for* me. When my husband left our home, I felt as if God had discarded me also. And when I've experienced subsequent disappointments, it was hard to *feel* God's love for me. The psalmist, battling unnamed enemies, asked God for a sign of His goodness. And I can testify that God is so faithful to answer that prayer. In my hardest seasons, God has sent beautiful signs of His goodness: a friend phones to check on my heart at just the right time; money that I need is provided; a word from the pulpit ministers to my heart; God's Spirit assures me of what is most true. Beloved, be bold to ask God for a sign of His goodness. You don't need to specify the form, but trust that God longs to comfort and help you. Then keep your eyes and ears open.

Lord, You have proven Yourself to be a comforter and helper. So I ask for a sign of Your goodness. Open my eyes to recognize Your presence, and open my ears to hear the words You are speaking to my heart. I put my wholehearted trust in You. Amen.

The Right to Be a Child of God

Yet to all who did receive him, to those who believed in his name, he gave the right to become children of God—children born not of natural descent, nor of human decision or a husband's will, but born of God. The Word became flesh and made his dwelling among us. We have seen his glory, the glory of the one and only Son, who came from the Father, full of grace and truth.

JOHN 1:12–14

What do you know about your earliest beginnings? Maybe you were a child that your mother and father hoped and prayed for. Or perhaps you were a surprise to them both! If the parents who bore you weren't able to care for you, you may have been raised by relatives or an adoptive family. Or maybe you never had a home that felt secure. The Gospel writer John—who is as much theologian as storyteller!—confirms that what is most true about your identity does not depend on how you came into the world. You are God's child because you have been born of God. That is what is *most true* about who you are. As a person who was adopted as an infant and later experienced the fracturing of my adoptive family, I treasure this assurance that, body and soul, I belong to God.

Father, I thank You that I am Your daughter. Before the world was made, You imagined me and You knit me together in a human womb. In body and soul, in life and in death, I belong to You. Amen.

The Child Who Was Lost Has Been Found

"The son said to him, 'Father, I have sinned against heaven and against you. I am no longer worthy to be called your son.' But the father said to his servants, 'Quick! Bring the best robe and put it on him. Put a ring on his finger and sandals on his feet. Bring the fattened calf and kill it. Let's have a feast and celebrate. For this son of mine was dead and is alive again; he was lost and is found.' So they began to celebrate."

Luke 15:21–24

When we stray from God, when we sin, the deceiver can whisper lies to our souls. Though they come in different forms, that sinister hiss often accuses: "God doesn't care for you"; "You are far from God"; "You're not worthy of love either human or divine." But Jesus describes a child who's gone astray but then pivots, repents, turns around to face his father. As Jesus is speaking, can you see the radiant face of that father? He is elated to have his boy home! He wants nothing more than to throw a party and celebrate the return of his beloved child. Sister, spend time today meditating on the face that joyfully receives you without any hesitation. You *are* the beloved child.

Father, I confess that I have been tempted to believe the enemy's lies. But Your truth has dispelled those lies and exposed what is most true: Your unbridled and unfailing love for me. Thank You for receiving and embracing me as Your daughter. Amen.

You're Invited to Be Fed

"Come, all you who are thirsty, come to the waters; and you who have no money, come, buy and eat! Come, buy wine and milk without money and without cost. Why spend money on what is not bread, and your labor on what does not satisfy? Listen, listen to me, and eat what is good, and you will delight in the richest of fare. Give ear and come to me; listen, that you may live."

Isaiah 55:1–3

Through the prophet Isaiah, God extends a glorious invitation. He invites everyone who is thirsty and hungry to drink and be fed. In this generous invitation, God also names a problem from which many of us suffer: we spend our money and energies on what doesn't truly satisfy. I'm not sure what that looks like in your life, but I see it all around me: the time we invest in social media, the money we pour into buying "stuff" we don't need, the energy we put into our appearances. Isaiah introduces us to a host who welcomes us to eat and drink without paying a dime! When we eat the bread God provides and when we drink His living waters, we are finally satisfied. Can you hear God's gentle invitation to you today?

Gracious God, good Provider, I hear Your voice inviting me to be fed by You. Quiet my heart as I feast on what You provide. Teach me to listen so that I may live. Amen.

You Will Fish for People

For he and all his companions were astonished at the catch of fish they had taken, and so were James and John, the sons of Zebedee, Simon's partners. Then Jesus said to Simon, "Don't be afraid; from now on you will fish for people." So they pulled their boats up on shore, left everything and followed him.

Luke 5:9–11

At the beginning of Jesus' ministry, before many people knew who He was, He wandered down to the sea's edge, where He met two pairs of brothers who were fishermen. Though they hadn't caught any fish, they obeyed Jesus' instruction to drop the nets *one more time*. When they lifted them, they were full of so many fish that the nets began to break! And in that odd encounter, their eyes were opened to recognize that Jesus was someone who was worth following. Something so powerful had transpired that what happens next doesn't even make sense: they left their business behind and followed Jesus. It's hard for us to understand, isn't it!? But the invitation from Jesus to fish for people was so compelling that all four men accepted without hesitation. How is Jesus calling you to follow Him today? And how will you respond to that invitation?

Jesus, like those four fishermen, I have encountered You and I believe that You are worth following. Empower me today to hear Your call and to respond with obedience to the sound of Your voice. Amen.

He Took Up Our Infirmities and Bore Our Diseases

When evening came, many who were demon-possessed were brought to him, and he drove out the spirits with a word and healed all the sick. This was to fulfill what was spoken through the prophet Isaiah: "He took up our infirmities and bore our diseases."
Matthew 8:16–17

Wouldn't it have been amazing to see Jesus perform the miracles we read about in the Gospels? He gave sight to a man who'd been born blind. He raised a widow's son from the dead. He healed a man who was paralyzed. He stopped a woman's interminable bleeding. As word got out, people began bringing their loved ones to Jesus to be healed. Although those being healed didn't yet understand who He was, Jesus was fulfilling Isaiah's prophecy that God's suffering servant would take up our infirmities and bear our diseases. He did the same for you and me in His death and resurrection. He gave His life so that we might be healed and redeemed from the power of sin and death in the world. Beloved, Jesus welcomes you to bring your hurts to Him.

Gracious Savior, I believe that You came to heal and redeem the world and that You came to heal and redeem me. Because I trust that You are good and faithful, I bring to You my physical, spiritual, and emotional hurts, believing that You are a good healer. Amen.

Your Friends Will Carry You to Jesus

They gathered in such large numbers that there was no room left, not even outside the door, and he preached the word to them. Some men came, bringing to him a paralyzed man, carried by four of them. Since they could not get him to Jesus because of the crowd, they made an opening in the roof above Jesus by digging through it and then lowered the mat the man was lying on. When Jesus saw their faith, he said to the paralyzed man, "Son, your sins are forgiven."

MARK 2:2–5

When Jesus was preaching inside a local building, people were packed inside and even listening in from outside! Four friends who'd been listening to Jesus believed that He could heal their friend. Their friend was paralyzed, and they knew that if they could get him before Jesus, he could be healed. That is what we call *big faith*. Doors blocked, windows crowded, these four carried their friend up to the roof! After tearing apart the roof to make an opening, they lowered him in front of Jesus using the mat he'd been lying on. Mark reports that Jesus *saw* their faith. Seeing their faith, He forgave the man's sin and then continued to heal his body. How have your friends brought you into the presence of Jesus?

God, thank You for the witness of these four friends who put their faith in Jesus. Equip me to be that friend who lifts, drags, and pulls my friends closer to You. Amen.

I Sought the Lord and He Answered

I sought the Lord, *and he answered me; he delivered me from all my fears. Those who look to him are radiant; their faces are never covered with shame.*
Psalm 34:4–5

When I've had a particularly tough week—a difficult parenting situation, a romantic disappointment, a challenging client, or a health concern—I often turn to my friends. I know the one who's not afraid to see my pain and reflect it back to me. I know the one who will get all fired up if I've been harmed or wronged in any way. I know the one who is going to deliver the very best joke at the right time. And I know who's available to just weep with me. While I believe my community is a good gift God has given me, sometimes I overlook my obvious Helper when I shoot off a text to a friend or call her for help. Yet the psalmist reminds me that when we seek the Lord, He answers. He delivers. This week, notice your impulse to find comfort in those around you. While you'll definitely want to share your life with the people who are closest to you, *begin* by seeking the Lord. Turn your face to God, and welcome Him to reign as your deliverer.

God, I thank You for Your steadfast, faithful presence. When I tip my eyes and ears to Your face, when I call on You with my voice, You answer! You deliver! Continue to quicken my heart to turn to You for what I most need. Amen.

I Have Come So That You May Have Life

"I am the gate; whoever enters through me will be saved. They will come in and go out, and find pasture. The thief comes only to steal and kill and destroy; I have come that they may have life, and have it to the full. I am the good shepherd. The good shepherd lays down his life for the sheep."

John 10:9–11

When Jesus identifies Himself as the Good Shepherd, the One who cares for His sheep, He contrasts Himself with the devil, whom He calls "the thief." It is really powerful language for the enemy of our souls! He also contrasts what the thief is about—stealing, killing, and destroying—with what He is about. And Jesus is clear, "I have come that they may have life, and have it to the full." I encourage you to hold on to this couplet this week. When you're faced with decisions, quietly and prayerfully ask God which choice—or which *gate*!—leads to life and which one leads to death and destruction. Beloved, you are the precious sheep Jesus came to save, and He is leading you into abundant life.

Good Shepherd, I believe that You are who You say that You are. Teach me to obey Your voice so that I might find real life in You. Help me to discern the wily ways of the thief who comes to steal, kill, and destroy. Amen.

Scripture Index

December 25, 2021

Dear Madeline,
Always remember that I love you more than all the stars in the sky. I am so proud and grateful for the sweet, kind girl who you are. As hard as it is to imagine – God loves you even more than I. You are indeed precious in His sight. ♡ Oma